past the wishing

Jen DeWeerdt

PUBLISHING

Published by Rockford First
www.rockfordfirst.com

All Biblical quotations, unless otherwise specified, are taken from the Holy Bible, New International Version®, NIV®. Copyright © 1973, 1978, 1984, 2011 by Biblica, Inc.™ Used by permission of Zondervan. All rights reserved worldwide. www.zondervan.com The "NIV" and "New International Version" are trademarks registered in the United States Patent and Trademark Office by Biblica, Inc.™

Scripture quotations from THE MESSAGE. Copyright © by Eugene H. Peterson 1993, 1994, 1995, 1996, 2000, 2001, 2002. Used by permission of Tyndale House Publishers, Inc.

Scripture quotations from the Holy Bible, New Living Translation, copyright ©1996, 2004, 2007, 2013 by Tyndale House Foundation. Used by permission of Tyndale House Publishers, Inc., Carol Stream, Illinois 60188. All rights reserved.

Scripture quotations from The Authorized (King James) Version. Rights in the Authorized Version in the United Kingdom are vested in the Crown. Reproduced by permission of the Crown's patentee, Cambridge University Press.

Scripture quotations marked (AMP) are taken from the Amplified Bible, Copyright © 1954, 1958, 1962, 1964, 1965, 1987 by The Lockman Foundation. Used by permission.

Text type is set in Adobe Caslon Pro

First Edition

ISBN: 978-0-692-40706-6

To my husband,
You've always believed I could
do far more than just wish.
All my love.

Contents

Chapter One:

The Lead-Foot Life

The bad news is time flies,
the good news is you're the pilot.

— *Michael Altshuler*

I am a chronic speeder. I know, I know, I'm not supposed to be a speed limit law-breaker, because not only am I a good Christian girl, but I am also a pastor. I am not supposed to be a speeder, but I am. Not only am I a chronic speeder, but I also have to admit there are times when I speed and I am fully aware of it. I'm in a hurry, I'm running late (I am seriously punctually challenged), I had to change a poopy diaper, or I forgot something, or, or, or—the possibilities are endless as to why. But then there are the times when I am speeding and I am completely unaware of how fast I'm going. I'm just going. *Fast.* Those are the times I glance down at the speedometer and see that I am going 60 in a 45 MPH zone. Yikes! What do I do? I slowly and discreetly apply the brakes rather than slamming on them…just in case there is a nice police officer around. I wouldn't want to tip anyone off to the fact I was just racing down this nice residential street, now would I? We've all been there. *(Right? Please tell me I'm not the only one!)*

Life can be a lot like this latter scenario. We're just speeding along, completely unaware of just how fast life is going. And then a moment comes where we look around and YIKES! Life is going faster than we want, but unlike a speeding car, it's sometimes difficult and complicated to put the brakes on the "crazy" of life and bring it down to a manageable pace.

I've discovered that it's nearly impossible to plan, focus, and dream for our lives when we are living what I would call a "lead-foot life"—a life that is governed by speed and busyness instead of thoughtful, prayerful planning. We see areas of our lives we would like to change; relationships we know need attention, daily disciplines that need addressing, but the exhausting lead-foot life keeps us from taking the time to make the necessary changes to bring about the kind of life we so desperately desire.

As we live our lead-foot lives…

We WISH our friendships were deeper.
We WISH our marriages had more romance.
We WISH our kids didn't play on the iPad as much.
We WISH our health was better and we exercised more.
We WISH we prayed more.
We WISH we had that degree.
We WISH we talked to that family member more.
We WISH we served in our community.
We WISH we read more.

Simply put, those who live lead-foot lives become wishers. Everything in life is a WISH, with no real effort ever put into making those wishes become reality. Ouch.

I hate this, but it's true! And I need to confess to you today that I am a WISHER.

In my heart I have been compiling a list of wishes: hopes and dreams that have taken a backseat to the things that scream for my immediate attention. My wishes range from deeply personal to simply pragmatic in nature. But they all speak to the person I know in my heart I want to be, to the health I want my relationships to have, to the depth I want in my spiritual walk, and to the fullness and brilliance I want my life to possess. These desires I hold so dear to my heart deserve to be more than wishes, and so do yours.

When we come to the realization that we are just wishers, there are many reactions we can have. We can become a martyr, thinking we are just a victim of our crazy lives and we can't do a darn thing about it. We can become paralyzed and overwhelmed by everything we would like to see changed. We can play the blame game, which we all know won't get us anywhere. We can be apathetic, knowing things could change, even *should* change, but we are unwilling to put forth the effort. We can hold a pity party, where we cry about it and invite other people to come cry with us. None of these scenarios will end with our desired result.

Might I suggest a different path? One that might take a little more time and thoughtfulness but is way more likely to take us where we want to go. Before we talk of the path, I want to be clear on something. I have not arrived when it comes to this journey. This book is being birthed out of my own daily struggle to move out of a crazy, lead-foot life, and into a life of meaning and purpose.

It was the late winter or early spring of 2014 when I began to sense a restlessness and discontentment with some areas of my life that I knew were just drifting—*maintaining*. Although my boys were all doing well, there were new parenting challenges that needed addressing. Although I had a great husband who was loving and supportive, there were new dimensions to my marriage of 18.5 years that I wanted to give thoughtful prayer and attention to. Although the church we were pastoring was gaining health and growth after a long seven-year battle, we knew much time, thought, prayer and strategy were needed as we entered into the next season. Although my health was decent, I was tired, lacked energy and knew I needed to change some things. Although the relationships with my family and friends were good, I desired to be a better aunt, sister, daughter, friend, and pastor.

Dare I say I wanted MORE out of life? The moment I type those words, I exhale a sigh of guilt. I already have so much…a good life, not a perfect life, but a good life. I guess a better way of putting words to my desire is to say I wanted to be *a better steward* of all I had been so graciously given.

In its noun form, a steward is "a person who manages another's property or financial affairs; a person who has charge of the household of another" (Dictionary.com).

I guess I've always thought of the word "steward" as a verb: "to act or serve as a steward," which is not as personal. But thinking of the word as a noun, as a kind of person, brought it home for me. I realized that I am not simply *to* steward (the verb) all God has given me, I AM A STEWARD. I am the person who manages another's property. I am the person, just the right person, to manage God's property. I truly believe that everything I have been given is a gift from God. I believe it 1,000 percent. So the "more" I find myself wanting isn't more stuff—not at all! That kind of "wanting more" takes us down an ugly path. No, this desire for more that I find in myself is all about doing MORE with what God has already given me.

James 1:16-17 says, "Don't be deceived my dear brother and sisters. Every good and perfect gift is from above, coming down from the Father of the heavenly lights, who does not change like shifting shadows." When we come to the realization we are stewards, caretakers of all God has given us, we will see that we must, absolutely must, take the time to let the foot off the gas pedal of our lives and focus on being the best steward we can be. Because in reality, it's not really about being the best wife, mom, friend, daughter, or pastor I can be, or being the best one *you* can be. It's about being the best steward of all God's property that He has placed in our care. What a new perspective!

In Matthew 25:14-30, Jesus tells a story that drives this point home:

> Again, the Kingdom of Heaven can be illustrated by the story of a man going on a long trip. He called together his servants and entrusted his money to them while he was gone. He gave five bags of silver to one, two bags of silver to another, and one bag of silver to the last—dividing it in proportion to their abilities. He then left on his trip.
>
> The servant who received the five bags of silver began to invest the money and earned five more. The servant with two bags of silver also went to work and earned two more. But the servant who received the one bag of silver dug a hole in the ground and hid the master's money.
>
> After a long time their master returned from his trip and called them to give an account of how they had used his money. The servant to whom he had entrusted the five bags of silver came forward with five more and said, "Master, you gave me five bags of silver to invest, and I have earned five more." The master was full of praise. "Well done, my good and faithful servant. You have been faithful in handling this small amount, so now I will give you many more responsibilities. Let's celebrate together!"
>
> The servant who had received the two bags of silver came forward and said, "Master, you gave me two bags of silver to invest, and I have earned two more." The master said, "Well done, my good and faithful servant. You have been faithful in handling this small amount, so now I will give you many more responsibilities. Let's celebrate together!"
>
> Then the servant with the one bag of silver came and said,

"Master, I knew you were a harsh man, harvesting crops you didn't plant and gathering crops you didn't cultivate. I was afraid I would lose your money, so I hid it in the earth. Look, here is your money back." But the master replied, "You wicked and lazy servant! If you knew I harvested crops I didn't plant and gathered crops I didn't cultivate, why didn't you deposit my money in the bank? At least I could have gotten some interest on it."

Then he ordered, "Take the money from this servant, and give it to the one with the ten bags of silver. To those who use well what they are given, even more will be given, and they will have an abundance. But from those who do nothing, even what little they have will be taken away. Now throw this useless servant into outer darkness, where there will be weeping and gnashing of teeth" (NLT).

Notice that the master never tells the servants—the stewards—how exactly to invest or manage what he entrusted to them. He leaves that up to the stewards. I find that odd, don't you? I mean, why doesn't he leave specific instructions? Isn't there an exact way he wants things done? I need more information! Rather than spelling it all out, this passage in the Bible makes it clear that the master entrusts his treasure to these stewards, and then he leaves on his trip. Can't you picture the stewards gathered around the master's caravan as it prepares to depart, asking questions like, "Umm, excuse me, Master? I need a little more information here. Can I get some clearer expectations? Maybe a check-list, a manual…anything!?!"

I relate to this moment; I ask these questions. I get nervous because I want to be a good steward! I want to please the Master. But just like these stewards, we often don't get the play-by-play instructions that we think we need. Why not? What about this: maybe, just maybe, the Master has entrusted each of us with what we have, because He's given us everything we need to steward His property. We can see this principle in action in the story. The master divided the treasure in proportion to the abilities of the servants, his stewards. Think about that. That means He has given you the ability, the resources, and the wisdom to handle exactly what He's placed in your care. To me, that's a humbling and empowering truth. I don't have to question whether or not I have it in me to care for what He's given me. The fact that I have these things to care for speaks to the truth that I *do* have the ability to care for them. He's left us in charge of His treasure, now it's time to get to work!

We know that the first two stewards went to work and both doubled their money by the time the master returned home. You know what? That "doubling" didn't just happen. I'm sure it took a lot of hard work and thoughtful planning to receive the "good and faithful" stamp of approval. We'll talk more about that later, but for now I want to focus on the third servant for a moment. You know, the one we don't want to be like? The one who lost it all and got thrown into outer darkness? Yeah, that one. I mean, what did he do that was so bad? So maybe he wasn't a risk-taker. Maybe he was just fearful. Maybe he doubted himself. Maybe he felt ripped off that he had gotten less than everyone else. Those are all valid feelings, right? Maybe not.

The problem with this little friend of ours is that as he begins to explain how he handled the master's treasure, he immediately starts in with excuses.

"I knew you were a harsh master."
"You have high standards."
"I was afraid."

Upon hearing the servant's excuses, the master calls him out, saying he is "wicked and lazy." When I first read this, it seemed overly harsh! Give the guy a break! But the truth is the master knew that his excuses were a cover up for his apathy and laziness. I am no different than this third servant sometimes. It's easy for me to come up with excuses as to why I'm not able to be a good and faithful steward of all God has given me. I blame fear, feelings, schedule, my past, or other people, but the bottom line is, if God has given it to me, I have what it takes to care for it all.

What I found ironic in this story are the similarities between the words used to describe both types of servants. The words that are used in the original language of Scripture to describe the "investing" of the first two servants are the words "to toil (as a task, occupation, etc.)" (Strong's Concordance). Meaning they worked hard at being stewards of what the master had given them. They toiled as if it was their job, their task, their occupation. I'm sure the work was difficult, time consuming, maybe even stressful. "Toil" isn't a light word in my opinion. Similarly, when the word "wicked" is used to describe the third servant, it is derived from a word meaning "to toil for daily subsistence" (Strong's Concordance). "Subsistence" means to support yourself at the minimum level; you have just enough to exist. So the third servant was toiling just enough to exist or survive. Either way, there is toil in life. We just get to choose which kind. We can either get our hands dirty by working hard or by burying our God-given ability. Today, I choose to toil for more than just existence or survival. I choose to toil for MORE.

We all know that in life there is the wrong kind of "more" and the right kind of "more." We're talking about the right kind here—the kind that creates eternal value. See, the first two servants in this story toiled for exactly that kind of more. They saw the value of what the Master had entrusted them with and then realized *they could add value.* Dear friends, God has so graciously handed us this one beautiful, crazy life, and now He says, "Let's see what you can add." So let's get to work! You and me! I'm ready to do the hard work, the intentional work, the time-consuming work, the get-your-hands-and-clothes-dirty kind of work to add value to what God has given me. In other words, I'm past the wishing, and I'm ready for the work.

So, where do we start? Moving past the wishing begins with inviting God into our journey. I know you may be reading this book in the privacy and quiet of your home, or maybe you're on a full plane with the person next to you sitting very close. Maybe you're sipping a latte in a busy coffee shop or sitting under a dryer in a salon with your hair full of aluminum strips. Wherever you may be, I want you to stop reading, dog-ear this page, close the book, take a few minutes and invite God

God has so graciously handed us this ONE beautiful, crazy life, and now HE says, "Let's see what you can add."

into this journey with you. Acknowledge that you need Him in the specific areas of your relationships, family, health, or profession. Just talk to Him for a while—don't lose focus. Remember you can talk to God like you are talking to a friend. You don't have to use flowery language or have the perfect words.

Dear Heavenly Father,
I take a moment and thank You for my friends. I pray they would sense Your presence even now as they pause to invite You into their journey of going past the wishing. I ask that You would lead and direct their daily steps. Give them wisdom and discernment as they take time to give intentional thought and action to this beautiful life You have given them. Give them the discipline and strength to see this journey through. In Jesus' name we pray. AMEN.

As we begin our journey together, here are some questions to ask yourself:

What are the wishes you want to turn into actions?
What are some of the excuses you need to remove in order to move past the wishing?

Take some time in the next few days to take your foot off the lead-foot life and talk to God about the MORE you want to add to your life.

Chapter Two:

You Complete Me

You don't cross my mind, you live in it.

-Anonymous

A few years back, Jer and I had the privilege of going to Paris, France, for a conference he was speaking at. As you can imagine, I had a difficult time deciding whether or not to go. I had to think it over for, say, two seconds! Who wouldn't jump at the chance to go to the City of Love? Before the conference started, we had some time to see the city. We walked, took the metro, and taxied throughout the city, all the while taking in the beautiful scenery of such a magnificent and historical place. Versailles, the Eiffel Tower, Notre Dame—it seemed every corner we turned held new views of timeless architecture and grandiose landscapes. As we ventured out one afternoon, we happened upon a walking bridge that crossed the Seine River. Both sides of the bridge had been outfitted with chain link fence which held thousands of locks of all shapes and sizes. Each lock had been engraved with personal messages and initials, carefully locked into place, and then the key was thrown in the Seine.

The Lover's Lock Bridge is not a new concept—there are quite a few worldwide—but I had never seen one before. Of course Jer and I had to buy a lock from the vendor who was selling over-priced, chintzy locks for folks just like us who couldn't wait to leave their mark on the Lover's Bridge in the middle of Paris. We borrowed a sharpie, wrote our initials, locked our lock and threw our key in the river symbolizing our ever and always love for one another. So romantic, right?

There is something powerful and intriguing about the concept of everlasting love. Poets and authors have penned about true, eternal love for thousands of years. Musicians have toiled over the lyrics to love songs and strived to match the perfect note to each heart-felt word. Artists have poured their hearts out on blank canvas trying to depict our human need for true, everlasting love. We were all made to long for true love. It's the way we were divinely designed. I want to speak to this need, this desire for true love, and what it means for our journey of moving past the wishing.

In Jeremiah 31:3 God is speaking to His people, and He states, "I have loved you with an everlasting love, I have drawn you with unfailing kindness." God is drawing us into a journey of change because of His everlasting love and unfailing kindness. Every challenge He will whisper to our hearts is done from a position of His deep love and commitment to us. He never speaks to us from a place of guilt, condemnation, and shame. The latter are always tactics of the enemy of our souls. Moving past the wishing will involve change, but the changes will be worked in our lives by a God who loves us with an everlasting love.

"Everlasting" means the vanishing point, out of mind, *always* (Strong's Concordance). God's love for us is eternal, having no end. In our finite minds, it is so hard to grasp the thought of something having no end, something that even though we may try as hard as we can to outrun it, just keeps going on forever. Do you know that you are fully loved, for all of time, no matter what? It is my prayer that you would know and experience this kind of deep, never-ending, everlasting love.

Would you do something? Would you take a deep breath and really think about the following statement? Block out distractions and meditate on it quietly. Don't be too quick to move on. Take a couple of minutes and put your focus on this thought:

I am fully loved, for all of time, no matter what.

You might be thinking—"What does understanding and knowing God's amazing love for me have to do with intentional living and moving past the wishing?" I truly believe if we can grasp the never-ending, all-encompassing love God has for us, the implications will be far-reaching and life-changing. Imagine what our lives would be like if we were to take every single step of our dear, precious life believing "I am fully loved, for all of time, no matter what." I would dare to say our steps would be more bold and sure; self-doubt would begin to fade and God-confidence would move to the forefront. We would begin to see exactly how our Master desires us to be good stewards: to add the "more" He is looking for from a position of acceptance and peace, instead of from a stance of fear, doubt, and striving. We would understand that God doesn't want us to add value to our lives because we aren't enough already, but because we *are* enough, and He trusts us to add value to the already priceless life He has given each one of us.

I talk to countless women and have heard countless stories of amazing, beautiful, talented, strong women who continually doubt their value and purpose in God. They wonder if they are loved by our Father God; they walk through life continually questioning their worth. I am emboldened to prayerfully remind us all that we cannot move forward if we continue to live in condemnation, fear, self-hate, and doubt. We must walk boldly in the truth that we are *fully loved, for all of time, no matter what* by our Creator God. Any thoughts contrary to such truth are directly from the enemy of our souls. Period. We need to silence him with the truth.

Imagine what our lives would be like if we were to take every single step of our dear, precious life believing "I am fully loved, for all of time, no matter what."

I wish I could sit across the table from you, look you straight in the eye and remind you of your value. I wish I could hide myself in your coat pocket, and every time you had a moment of self-hate or doubt, I could pop up and remind you what God really thinks about you. But I can't. You have to do that. You have to be the one to take captive your thoughts and make them subject to the promises of God. You need to be the one to speak truth to the lies. No one can do that for you.

Times and the human psyche haven't changed much since when the New Testament was written. Even the Apostle Paul had to encourage and remind the early church of Ephesus about this basic, but important truth. In Ephesians 3:17-19 Paul states:

> I pray that from his glorious, unlimited resources he will empower you with inner strength through his Spirit. Then Christ will make his home in your hearts as you trust in him. Your roots will grow down into God's love and keep you strong. And may you have the power to understand, as all God's people should, how wide, how long, how deep, and how high his love is. May you experience the love of Christ, though it is too great to understand fully. Then you will be made complete with all the fullness of life and power that comes from God (NLT).

I love the progression of this verse, ending with "you will be made complete." What a strong word. This is what we all desire, correct? To be *complete*. If only it was as easy as having a Jerry McGuire moment when the Tom Cruise of our lives busts through the front door and says, "You complete me." And we say, "You had me at hello." Oh, Tom, you'll always be Maverick from *Top Gun* to me. I digress. The truth is we don't need to be "more" or to *do* "more" to be complete. What we need is the power to understand God's love! This is the truth Paul is writing about; let's follow Paul's thought process for a moment.

He starts this passage with a prayer that the recipients of his letter would be empowered with inner strength through God's Spirit and that Christ would make his HOME in their hearts as they trust him.

Christ wants to be at home in our hearts. That sounds like a cute idea, but in reality that could be really frightening! I mean, let's talk about our homes for a minute…. Okay, I won't make you go there, I'll just talk about my home for a minute. There are five people who live in my home: Jer, myself, Caden (15), Connor (13), and Pax (3).

Parenting our three boys is a crazy, amazing, adventure which also comes with its fair share of challenges. Being married to Jer is amazing, but we have challenges just like any other couple that has been married for almost 20 years. In our home we see the good, the bad, and the ugly of each person. Home is where we see the struggles, hardships, and low points as well as the joys, accomplishments, and high points of each member of the family. Home can be messy, smelly, common. The place where we let our guard down. The place where we can all be ourselves.

Do you know that Christ wants to be right in the middle of our crazy, imperfect, adventurous, messy life? He wants to be at home in our hearts. He wants to be right in the middle of the good, bad, and ugly—our spiritual bed head and morning breath as well as our accomplishments and joys. After all, isn't it in our homes where our families see it ALL—every little thing? And isn't it the fact that they still love us anyway what makes us feel truly loved? Isn't that what HOME should really mean? Being both fully known and fully loved? This is what God is offering! Do you know God sees it all, and He still loves us fully, for all of time, no matter what?

Christ will make His home in our hearts as we trust in Him, Paul says. Trust is a continual choice, and making the day-by-day, minute-by-minute choice to trust Him is what will help establish our roots and keep us strong. Trust Him in the good times, the hard times, the easy times, the fun times, the difficult times—trust in Him all of the time. That's when our roots grow deep, and deep roots equal the strength to move past the wishing and into the more!

Paul then continues his prayer by saying, "And may you have the power to understand, as all God's people should, how wide, how long, how deep, and how high his love is." "The POWER to understand…" these are not apathetic, laid-back words. To grasp God's love for us is not some passive, weak-willed act, but rather a purposeful, determined choice to wrestle down the truth of God's love for us and not let it go easily. It must be pinned down. Sometimes truth has to be forcefully possessed, because that is what is needed to kick us out of the comfort that has been provided by our insecurities. It is Paul's passion and heart that we have the strength to seize the truth. He knows it is worth the necessary effort.

There have been countless times in my life when I have fed on lies such as "You are not enough," "God doesn't love you," "You can't do anything right," and the like. Listening to these lies for so long caused me to become obese on falsehood and consequently too weak to put up a fight for the truth. At some point, my friends, we have to stand up on the inside and decide that although sometimes it may be easier to wallow in lies, we were made for more. We need to start swinging with all we have in us for the Truth of who we are in Christ and the value that He has placed on us. Some of us have been fighting so hard to please God and to be accepted by Him, and what we really need to be doing is fighting hard to accept and believe the truth of His love for us.

Paul wants us to have the strength to comprehend "how wide, how long, how deep, and how high his love is." How can something be so vast and large, but so difficult for us to see and know? It's kind of like the galaxy we live in. It is infinitely bigger than us, and it's so big, we can't understand it or fathom it. Maybe that's why it's so hard to comprehend and pin down God's love for us. It's almost too big. It is infinitely wide, long, deep, and high.

Wide enough to include everyone,
Long enough to span all of time,
Deep enough to be unfathomable,
High enough to be beyond the reach of any foe to deprive us of.

What does this mean for us? Right here, right now, in our mundane, normal, everyday lives?

We yell at our kids.
We are impatient.
We watch too much TV.
WE ARE LOVED.
We are addicted to social media.
We harbor bitterness.
We are judgmental.
WE ARE LOVED.
We lack self-control.
We are mean to others.
We are materialistic.
WE ARE LOVED.
We are hurt.
We are broken.
We have been abused.
WE ARE LOVED.
We have abused.
We self-medicate.
We have secrets…we want no one to EVER find out.
WE ARE LOVED.
We have a dark side.
We carry shame and regret.
We are selfish.
WE ARE LOVED.

Period.

Maybe it's hard for us to grasp this kind of limitless love because our love, human love, has limits. Our love is only deep and wide enough to include certain people—the ones who think like us, the ones who don't make us uncomfortable in their beliefs, and the ones who basically do things the way we want them done. Our love is only long and wide enough to last a certain amount of time—until we've had enough, until we've been hurt, or until they've just gone too far. Your love has limits, my love has limits and often we view God's love for us through the lens of how we love ourselves and others. Ouch. No wonder Paul was letting his readers know he was praying they would be able to comprehend the extent of the Father's love for them.

The reality is we all need to hear the truth about God's real, unfailing, unending, more-than-enough love for us over and over and over again. This is true whether you have been a follower of Jesus Christ since you were a small child, or you are just beginning your journey of seeking truth. It is true whether you've had a great life, made perfect decisions and are currently living your dream, or if your life has been hard, either because of some of your decisions or because of the choices of someone else. Or maybe you're somewhere in between. No matter where we come from or what our current situation is, He asks us to trust in His unfailing love—to fight hard to believe and know it.

Paul doesn't stop there; he takes his prayer a step further and asks that we would "experience the love of Christ, though it is too great to understand fully." To experience means to be aware of and to feel. Yep, to feel! Dare I say that God's love should be felt as an emotion? Yes! I know that feelings have sometimes been labeled as the "F" word, and while it is true we can't let our feelings dictate our lives, we are human, and feelings are a part of how we are wired up. My husband and I have been married for almost twenty years—oh my, that is a long time! How can I be that old? Anyway, there have been plenty of times where the *feelings* of love we had towards each other were strong, passionate, and undeniable. Other times we knew that we loved each other deeply even though we weren't experiencing the *feelings*, the same butterflies as when we first started dating or early in our marriage. All that to say, I echo Paul's prayer for you—may you experience the love of Christ, though it is too great to understand fully!

A few years back, I was going through a difficult time where I was feeling very defeated. I was being hard on myself, I couldn't do anything right, and I felt like God was distant. One night as I was laying in bed, the room was dark, Jer was sleeping peacefully beside me, I got on my phone, opened my YouVersion Bible app and started reading. Now, I could have done a lot of other things in that moment, but I chose to open the Word of God, and you can too! Psalm 52:8 stood out to me, "But I am like an olive tree flourishing in the house of God; I trust in God's unfailing love for ever and ever." I'm sure I had read this verse many times before, but this time it stuck out to me. Yes! I am like a tree that is flourishing. I am not withering, I am prospering, I am growing. God, I TRUST in your unfailing love for ever and ever. I don't trust in my feelings, I don't trust in my doubt, I don't trust in what I think about myself—I trust what you think about me. I trust in your unfailing love.

I began to think about that verse over and over and over again. I fell asleep thinking of those words, and I woke up thinking about them. As I was walking through the days and weeks to follow, every time I encountered a feeling or thought that wasn't lining up with this truth, I would go back to this verse and align my thinking and my feelings to it. As I did this continually, I began to feel a sense of the reality of God's love settle in my heart.

We must carve time out of our busy schedules to spend time in His presence. That can look as simple as talking to God in prayer while driving your car, putting on some worship music as you work around the house, or sitting down to read His Word before you start your day. When I take a truth about God's love from His Word and carry it with me throughout the day…meditating on it…and calling it to remembrance…it sinks in deeply and comes to life. It may not look or feel like a strong emotion, but rather a steady assurance that settles in your heart, bringing peace and a confidence in God's love for you.

One of my favorite scriptures of all time is Ephesians 3:20, "God can do anything, you know—far more than you could ever imagine or guess or request in your wildest dreams! He does it not by pushing us around but by working within us, his Spirit deeply and gently within us" (MSG). This is a very famous verse, it is often quoted in churches, printed on t-shirts, penned in greeting cards, and sometimes tattooed on skin. It is powerful, faith-filled, and reassuring. I believe this scripture is so well-loved because it speaks to the desire for MORE that is inside so many of us. The promises spoken in this verse are true for us today!

God wants do far more in our lives than we could ever imagine or guess or request in our wildest dreams! He wants us to move past the wishing even more than we want to. He has a grand adventure that He is beckoning us to take with Him! When I was in college, a group of my girlfriends and I took a road trip to Florida—in January, which is the perfect time to get away from the Midwest winter. I will never forget piling into one of the girls' red convertible and spending long evenings cruising around in the warm Florida weather. If you have ever experienced having your best friend pull up to your house, windows down, music pumping, horn honking for you to come out and go paint the town, then you can picture the heart of God here—He is standing at the door of your heart, calling for you to come out and join Him in a life of MORE! He is inviting each one of us to experience the anything-is-possible life that comes by His Spirit moving gently and deeply within us. Ironically, Paul penned these words of MORE immediately following his heartfelt prayer for the church of Ephesus to know, grasp, understand, comprehend and experience the love of God! **Could it be when we receive, believe, and trust in God's love, we are then poised for God to do the impossible?**

I think so! I have seen this to be true in my life, and I believe it will be proven true in yours.

This is our starting point, girls! Everything God asks of us from this point on comes through the filter of understanding and believing we are deeply loved, for all of time, no matter what. There is really nothing to lose here. We are now armed with the truth and we are ready to move past the wishing. Let the adventure begin.

Here is a little something that will help to get the truth of God's love working in your life.

Take these verses and begin to meditate on them. Meditating isn't a weird, mystical exercise, rather it is a spiritual discipline that will help work off the flabbiness from the lies we have been feeding on. Let's get in shape, girls. Let's know who we are, so that we can be ready for this grand God-adventure we have been called to!

"He remembered us in our weakness. *His faithful love endures forever.*"
Psalm 136:23 (NLT)

"And I ask him that with both feet planted firmly on love, you'll be able to take in with all followers of Jesus the extravagant dimensions of Christ's love. Reach out and experience the breadth! Test its length! Plumb the depths! Rise to the heights! Live full lives, full in the fullness of God."
Ephesians 3:18-19 (MSG)

"The faithful love of the Lord never ends! His mercies never cease. Great is his faithfulness; his mercies begin afresh each morning."
Lamentations 3:22-23 (MSG)

"God's love, though, is ever and always, eternally present to all who fear him."
Psalm 103:17a (MSG)

"For even if the mountains walk away and the hills fall to pieces, My love won't walk away from you, my covenant commitment of peace won't fall apart. The God who has compassion on you says so."
Isaiah 54:10 (MSG)

"None of this fazes us because Jesus loves us. I'm absolutely convinced that nothing—nothing living or dead, angelic or demonic, today or tomorrow, high or low, thinkable or unthinkable—absolutely *nothing* can get between us and God's love because of the way that Jesus our Master has embraced us."
Romans 8:38-39 (MSG)

"But you, O God, are both tender and kind, not easily angered, immense in love, and you never, never quit."
Psalm 86:15 (MSG)

Chapter Three:

Team Brave

If you want to go fast, go alone.
If you want to go far, go together.

— *African Proverb*

The catalyst for this book was a rather unassuming meeting with friends that took place in May 2014. I believe that every chapter in this book contains truths and concepts that will embolden and equip us to move past the wishing. But this chapter holds the foundational, God-inspired idea that if we choose to bravely apply and then tenaciously see it through, it has the potential to mark our journeys with Christ in a truly significant way.

It was a warm day in May when a small group of girls and I gathered around a table at our local Starbucks to discuss some creative aspects for our upcoming Original Women's Conference happening the following April 2015. We sat around sipping our coffee, laughing at each other's comical stories of how our morning routines had unfolded. This beautiful crew consisted of Lori Eickhoff, Trina McNeilly, Lisa Seaton, and myself. As our meeting went on, we began to talk about the design, content, and message of the promotional magazine for conference 2015, and what unfolded was an incredibly Divine Moment which set the course for a journey which would profoundly impact each of our lives. As we began to discuss what we wanted the upcoming conference to be about, we found ourselves discussing what we as individuals wanted to be about. One by one we ended up sharing how there were dreams, goals, aspirations, and ideas that each of us had for our lives—many of which were just wishes right now. Nothing, or very little, was being done about them. In the busyness and craziness of our lead-foot lives, we were each left with a mounting, muddled list of goals, regrets, wants, and needs that were just sitting on the back burner of an already full life.

As we continued to share with deep honesty, the hustle and bustle of the coffee shop became muted background noise to an oh-so-important moment in time. We all leaned in to listen intently to one another and huddled close for this holy moment that included a few tears, napkins as tissue, and the occasional giggle as we realized this was all happening in the most unlikely of places at the most unlikely of times, and isn't that just like our God.

One of the observations we gathered from our vulnerable sharing was an undercurrent of fear. Many of the hopes and dreams we were sharing were things that had been looked at, contemplated, and then rejected because of an overwhelming fear of failure, fear of being hurt, or fear of not being good enough. So they were left to simmer over a steady flame of excuses and some perhaps topped with a lid of apathy. Well, we were done with that. We were ready to confront our fears head-on with the strength of friends. To this end, we founded what we fondly call Team Brave.

The word TEAM is powerful. It denotes you are not alone. When one member of the team is weak, the other members come alongside; they help, encourage, and give strength. They speak truth when confusion has set in and clarity is needed. They provide the accountability that is needed to accomplish the goals you have. They help lift your arms when you are weary and share the burden when life gets too heavy. They cheer you on as you run your race.

Those who know me well know that I am a crazy sports fanatic—I am a self-described super fan. When people come to our house for a big game, they come not to watch the sporting event, but to watch my enthusiastic antics. My favorite show to watch is SportsCenter on ESPN. I can be found watching it nightly, even when Jer is out of town. (I probably have issues.) With all that said, I have always loved the idea of team. I love watching a group of people, with different backgrounds, talents, and abilities, come together to achieve something great. It's not about the one undeniably talented person, but it's about the team that understands they need each other to accomplish great things.

Teams of people have climbed mountains, rowed across oceans, cycled over multiple countries —I venture to say that nothing of great significance has ever been accomplished solely by one person all alone. There is always a team of people in the background. Even the marathon runner, golfer, or cyclist who compete in a race alone, have been backed by a faithful team of trainers and experts who have helped them make it to the point of competition. Team doesn't make the task easier, but it does make it possible.

God is very clear in His Word that we are better together. Ecclesiastes 4:9-12 states, "Two are better than one, because they have a good return for their labor: If either of them falls down, one can help the other up. But pity anyone who falls and has no one to help them up. Also, if two lie down together, they will keep warm. But how can one keep warm alone? Though one may be overpowered, two can defend themselves. A cord of three strands is not quickly broken."

If we know this to be true, that TEAM is better than being alone, why do we so quickly push off the idea of true, meaningful, honest-talk friendships? Yes, some of us have been burned before. But it's like I've heard my husband say—"Just because you got a bad haircut, doesn't mean you stop getting them." You find a new hairdresser! You find someone you can trust. Yes, it can be scary being honest and vulnerable with a small group of people. But what's the alternative? To live life alone? In an honest moment, we know that really doesn't work. When we live in isolation, it's impossible to flourish because we were designed to live in community.

I am a pretty guarded person. I've always been fearful of saying the wrong thing or saying something incorrectly. I tend to just clam up and keep to myself when it comes to the deeper things of my life. A venture like Team Brave is a challenge for me. In fact, I think it is a challenge for all of us. On our lists of goals, which I will speak of shortly, one of the items we all listed was having a group such as ours that met consistently. Why would that be on our lists? Because we know it's important, but it doesn't come easy. It can be scary to commit to opening up your life in this way, we are all really busy, and we knew it would take time and consistent effort.

There are many excuses we can give for not being part of a team.

> *What if people don't accept me?*
> *I'm not a people person.*
> *I don't like to share honestly with people.*
> *I have trust issues.*
> *People bother me.*
> *I don't have time.*
> *I tried that once and it didn't work out.*
> *I'm shy.*
> *I'm too old.*
> *Women are too catty—I get along better with men.*

Well, enough of the excuses. The time is now. To move past the wishing we must move past our excuses. No matter how young or old you are, begin a purposeful journey to form your own Team Brave. I can't tell you how excited I am to see how this concept can change your life! Let's get to work.

Once again I want you to pause in your reading and spend a little time in thought. Right where you are, take a few minutes and start thinking about who YOU, yes you, can begin a Team Brave group with. You may not come back to reading this chapter for another three days, and that is okay. Thoughtfully pause and ask God to whisper to your heart who you are to form your group with. I honestly believe this may be the single greatest key to moving past the wishing—so this is your incredibly important homework assignment!

Let's make our first act of intentional living be a purposeful and forthright pursuit of forming a Team Brave.

Some ideas for my TEAM BRAVE:

_____

_____

_____

_____

_____

If this list was hard to make, or if you are still staring at these blanks, wondering who in the world could be on a Team Brave with you… perhaps you need to start by putting yourself in positions to meet new people, people who may become the members of your Team Brave. Attend that Bible study you've been meaning to get to. Introduce yourself to the ladies who sit near you at church, Sunday after Sunday. Go out to coffee with them! Join a volunteer team at your church and get to know some new people while serving together. Try out a life group through your church. Start a life group of your own! Step out into situations that will allow you to meet other women who, just like you, are wanting to get MORE out of life!

The beauty of this crazy idea of Team Brave is that it isn't limited to a group of people who are exactly the same. Our Team Brave is an unlikely, diverse group of girls who have decided to journey through life together on purpose. Your Team Brave won't look exactly like any other Team Brave. The key is to pull together a group of people who will commit to honest, open-hearted conversation, challenge one another in good ways, love and pray for one another, encourage, encourage, encourage, laugh, cry, and adventure together!

THE LISTS

Back to our meeting at Starbucks. At the end of our meeting together, we knew that this was just the beginning. This wasn't just going to be a one-time, nice, emotional conversation that took place between girlfriends that would be chalked up as a nice memory. We were ready to do something. We all committed to jump on the journey of intentional living together and just see where it would take us. The plan was to meet together again in two weeks, each of us armed with a list of goals broken down into three areas: Adventure, Personal, and Professional/Ministry. These were the areas that we naturally found a number of things that were merely wishes, and we weren't going to let them stay that way.

On Wednesday, June 4, we met again, this time with the sweet addition of my lovely personal assistant, Elisabeth (Liz) Willard, who was unable to attend the first meeting where Team Brave was formed. Each of us came with our Brave goals in hand—our very personal, raw, heartfelt goals. For me, knowing what to put on my list wasn't too hard to figure out. It was actually writing them down that took guts and thoughtfulness. I'm not going to lie, I felt a pressure as I wrote them down. Most of these things seemed way too big for me. Daunting tasks emotionally, spiritually, and physically. Once I wrote them down and then shared them, I was going to be held accountable to see them through. I think we all felt this pressure to some extent.

But along with the pressure came an excitement! We were doing this. We were really doing this! Those things we had thought about, dreamed of, maybe even felt guilt over were going to be taken off the back burner and placed at the forefront. It was a beautiful day, so we sat outside at the same Starbucks where this journey had begun. We shared our goals and a little background on each of them. We laughed, all of us nervously, as we discussed our Adventure goals of skydiving and running a half marathon together. There were some tears as we shared reasons for some of the deeply personal goals we had set. Broken relationships, hurt, infertility, family pain, disappointment were common themes through our lists. There were also smiles and anticipation as we spoke of our ministry and professional goals. We ended by praying for one another and committed to meeting once a month to catch up, go over our goals and support each other in our endeavors. We formed a text thread that over the months has been filled with updates, prayer requests, and celebrations of our journey together. Life-changing and life-giving are understatements.

This journey was something God had so sweetly been preparing me for. About a month leading up to our initial meeting where this all started, I felt God had been asking me to step out in some areas I knew were going to be difficult for me. I knew God was tugging at my heart saying, "Jen, I want you to make an intentional attempt to expose your heart to the things that make it ache and just see what I will do." I felt this so strongly that I pulled out my phone and typed an email to myself with that very line. That email, dated April 24, 2014, still sits in my inbox today.

The challenge God gave to me is the same I now give to you. I want you to make an intentional attempt to expose your heart to the things that make it ache and just see what He will do. If we want to be wild participants of our dear, precious lives, we will have to encounter circumstances, feelings, and challenges that launch us out of our comfort zones.

Make an intentional attempt to expose YOUR HEART to the things that make it ache, and just SEE what God will do.

Once you've gathered your Team Brave, your next step is to tackle listing out your goals. Below I am sharing a few of the goals from our Team Brave just to give you an idea of how it worked for us. We were a diverse group of women and so our lists are as different as our lives. I work at the church, am a pastor's wife, and have three children. Lisa and Liz both married within the last few years and have no children as of yet, and they both work at Rockford First. Trina is married with four children and works from her home. Lori is married with the hopes of children in the near future and is a small business owner.

So let's take a look at some of our goals:

ADVENTURE
- Skydiving (Jen's wild idea that we decided we would all do together)
- Scuba, parasail or surf (Trina)
- Road trip to the West Coast with my husband (Liz)
- Half marathon (Lisa's long-time dream we decided to do together)
- Summiting three 14,000 foot peaks with my husband (Lori)

PERSONAL
- Invest more into my relationship with my Dad (Jen)
- Lose 30lbs by my 30th birthday (Lori)
- Read more (Lisa)
- Get strong, build muscles, be healthy (Trina)
- Have a real conversation and spend quality time (dinner, coffee, whatever) with my mom and sister every six weeks (Jen)
- Start a family...keep trying naturally and also work on finalizing adoption details by the end of this year (Lori)
- Learn more about my city (Liz)
- Find something fun to do with my older boys once a month (Jen)
- Spend more time intentionally and strategically pouring into people (Lisa)
- Write...I used to journal all the time and haven't in the past few years (Lori)
- No "screens" in bed (Liz)

As I am sure you can understand, the nature of some of our personal goals required that we keep them in confidence.

MINISTRY/PROFESSIONAL
- Volunteer at Walter Lawson Children's Home (Jen & Liz)
- Prison ministry (Trina)
- Get involved in Big Brother/Big Sister (Lisa)
- Put together floral workshops for local retirement centers (Lori)
- Start up a consistent life group (Lisa)
- Invite my neighbors to church (Liz)
- Continue writing and putting together messages; not doubting what God has placed on my heart and doing the hard and heart work of getting my thoughts and messages out of me and down on paper (Jen)
- When I have something to share—say it (Trina)
- Write more. I love doing it. It's just taking the time, and having my heart and mind open to whatever it is that God wants to show me (Lisa)

Let me explain why we chose these topics.

ADVENTURE GOALS
First of all, why did we decide to set some adventurous goals? Well, simply put, we were Team Brave, and we were going to do some things that scared us to death! Things that were "bucket list" worthy. Things we didn't think physically we could accomplish. Things that pushed us beyond our limits and what we were comfortable with. Things that for us would usually begin with "I could never..." or "I've always wanted to...." These adventurous goals were a physical reflection of what we were going to be doing in our personal and professional/ministry goals. We were taking a leap on many levels on this journey together.

On a completely different note, these adventurous, crazy ideas we were going to do together were just FUN, too! We were going to be tackling some big-ticket items emotionally, relationally, and calling-wise in other areas, so we needed a little comic relief! We just needed a good laugh, even if it was a seriously nervous laugh. The really amazing part about these goals is that we walked away with some major, meaningful life lessons I am excited to share with you later in the pages of this book.

As you and your Team Brave choose your Adventure Goals, I encourage you to have some you do together and some you do alone or with someone else you love. Something powerful happens when you choose to do something you have to work towards together as a team. You each have different experiences, perspectives, emotions, and life-lessons you are learning along the way. These are priceless times and memories that will be forever etched in your mind.

PERSONAL GOALS

Our personal goals were just that, deeply personal. These were the raw, difficult, brutally honest, and extremely intimate areas of our lives we knew needed attention, and we were finally willing to do something about them. They weren't pretty. Most of these items were obvious, but difficult to admit to anyone. Although deeply personal, some of the steps we had to take to see the change we desired were very practical and non-glamorous. They ranged from taking a step towards forgiveness, to practicing discipline in our physical health or spiritual habits, or to tending to broken relationships that had sat neglected for years.

MINISTRY/PROFESSIONAL

These goals were others-centered and missional: goals that used our talents and gifts to help spread the Good News about His great love for every person. Team Brave was about more than making lists based on "I want to do all these things that are essentially about ME growing." (It is a good thing to do, but we knew we couldn't stop there because it wouldn't be the full measure of MORE.) It was important to make goals that pushed us to look outside of ourselves. As we were making our lists, we also found this was a good place to create some goals where we would be investing and sharing some of the gifts, talents, and drives God had placed within each of us. As we formed our lists, we knew there were ways we wanted to push ourselves to grow, whether that was writing more, studying further, practicing encouragement, or better utilizing a skill we had.

Now, I need to be really honest with you. The idea of this can sound a bit romanticized—that forming a Team Brave and implementing it will be an easy fix to moving past the wishing, and, well, it just isn't. It's not like every time we met together it felt like we were floating on clouds, the stars were aligning, and we felt cosmically connected. This is the farthest thing from the truth. In fact, our monthly meetings together were sometimes mundane, sometimes one or two people couldn't come due to kids or schedule conflicts; sometimes our moments together felt deep, sometimes they didn't.

Team Brave | Lisa, Lori, Jen, Trina & Liz

Starting a journey like Team Brave is just like any other journey you would take. If you wanted to make a road trip to Mount Rushmore or Niagara Falls, there would be moments when the view was breathtaking, exciting, and new. Other times, which is most of the time, it's just the rhythm of the creases in the road as you drive with cruise control on. The landscape goes rolling by, seemingly unchanging. It's the same view out the window, but even in the mundane, you are getting to your destination. Remember, the great part of this journey is the company you will get to keep along the way! I'm praying you have an amazing road trip with your Team Brave. That is what this book is all about!

It's time to do the work to move past the wishing! If you haven't already begun putting your Team Brave together, do so now! Send those texts, make those calls, set a day and a time, and break out your goal sheets!

Chapter Four:

Boy, Was He Right

For I know the plans I have for you says the
Lord, plans to prosper you and not to harm
you, plans to give you a hope and a future.

— *Jeremiah 29:11*

I think most of us are tempted to believe we can't move past the wishing until our circumstances are exactly how we want them. We are waiting until our husband has turned into Prince Charming, our kids actually listen to us, the sickness has been healed, we have perfect friends, we don't feel depressed anymore, we have the perfect job. We all too often pray that God would change our circumstances, instead of praying that God would give us the courage to be strong and courageous right in the middle of whatever circumstance we find ourselves in. We've all found ourselves in these moments—praying the trouble or hard times away. Yes, even me, a pastor! The truth is, moving past the wishing has nothing to do with our circumstances. One of the most incredible lessons I've learned about not wishing the tough times

Don't be tempted to believe we can't move past the Wishing until our circumstances are exactly how we want them.

away, but embracing where God has placed me and what He's entrusted to me is in the journey with our third son, Paxton.

In January 2011, I was preparing to lead a mission trip to Chiang Mai, Thailand, with a team of amazing women from our church. We were going to be working with our dear friends, Mike and Carol Hart, along with their entire team at ZOE Children's Home. This was my second trip to this amazing home where God continues to heal and restore children who were at risk or rescued out of the horrors of human trafficking and slavery.

As you might imagine, much preparation goes into these ministry trips. We do ministry and human trafficking awareness in villages, share Bible lessons in churches, share the Good News of Jesus in schools, minister, and just plain have a blast with our ZOE family. In the middle of all of the prayer and preparation for our ministry, God so sweetly began weaving together a theme for us. So many God-moments pointed us to the verse in Jeremiah 29:11, "For I know the plans I have for you says the Lord, plans to prosper you and not to harm you, plans to give you a hope and a future". I was so excited to see how God was going to use this theme in our times of ministry. Little did I know how deeply I was going to be living by this promise in the weeks and months to come. But God knew, and He was using this time to drill this message home, planting it deeply into my heart.

We left on January 18, 2010. All throughout our two weeks in Thailand, it was clear that God was preparing me for something great. The entire trip was one big encouragement and confirmation that God had big, amazing plans for me, my family, and my ministry. The year leading up to this trip had been significant for me. I was starting to hit my stride and find my confidence in what God had called me to do. Where fear and insecurity had once set up shop, strength and boldness were now at work. I knew God was placing messages in my heart that needed to be shared, that He had asked me to lead, and for the first time in my life, I knew I could do it.

I landed home on January 31, 2010, ready to take on the world. But before one takes on the world, she has to kiss and, well, you know what, with her hot hubby after being gone for two weeks! Let's just say that we call our son, Paxton, our "Welcome home from Thailand, Baby, baby." It was mid-February when I had that "Hmmmm, I think I might be late" moment, and three pregnancy tests later it was definitely a yes. We were in shock. This was not in the plans. I mean, our boys were nine and ten for crying out loud! By the time the baby would be born, there would be nearly a decade between kids. I would be having a kindergarten graduation and high school graduation in the same year. I was going to be thirty-eight and Jer forty-two when the baby would arrive.

Oh, and remember that stride I was talking about? Well, forget that now. I felt like I had just gotten pushed out of my lane, sprained my ankle, and then fallen flat on my face. I know children are a blessing, but I'm just being honest here. I was ready to change the world, step into some amazing dreams and plans I had for my life, and now I felt things had changed. Plus, adding a baby to an already crazy ministry and family schedule was not going to be easy, and we knew it. Sleepless nights, nursing, dirty diapers, all on top of having two middle school boys. Awesome.

Within a few days of that final positive pregnancy test, we left for a family trip to Tucson. There's nothing like a little time away and some sunshine in February to warm the soul and bring some perspective. During our trip, we creatively revealed the news to Caden and Connor that they were going to be big brothers. The joy on their faces and their undeniable, overwhelming excitement became contagious and before we knew it, Jer and I were ecstatic about our new addition. Phone calls were made to family members and friends. Emails and texts were sent to friends near and far. Just about everyone thought we were joking.

Other than the not-so-welcome visitors of nausea and her cousin, losing your lunch…daily, the first eighteen weeks of my pregnancy went well. I was healthy, baby was healthy. Around eighteen weeks, I began spotting and bleeding, which started a series of some pretty scary moments – one of which included an episode of significant bleeding as we were flying over the Atlantic Ocean headed to see our friends, Steve and Charlotte Gambill, in Bradford, England. Upon landing in Brussels, Belgium, for our layover, we immediately changed our flights and hopped on the first flight headed home. A couple of emergency room visits and trips to the doctor revealed a low-lying placenta, which was the cause for the bleeding. Thankfully, this was not life-threatening to the baby, and we breathed a sigh of relief. The upside of having so many ultrasounds and medical visits was that we were able to find out we were having a BOY!! We were thrilled. I would remain the queen of my castle.

In the midst of the journey to discover why I was bleeding, my OB had ordered a level two ultrasound at the department of Maternal Fetal Medicine at a local hospital. The morning of the appointment, I assured Jer that he did not need to attend this visit with me, since we had already diagnosed the source of the bleeding through our previous medical visits. I headed to the hospital for my appointment, excited to get another peek at the growing baby in my belly. It just so happened that my sister, Eileen, was working at the hospital that day, so she slipped away to be with me. Any excuse to see her new little nephew!

We entered the procedure room and got situated. The technician came in and began prepping for the test, making small talk and bustling around. Then she said something I will never forget. "So, you're here today because of the spots that were found on the heart and the bowel of the baby." She kept talking, but I didn't hear another word. My sister and I looked at each other in complete confusion. I was speechless. Words cannot capture the emotions that flood through a parent's heart when they hear that their child might be in danger. The technician had continued to talk about the procedure; she mentioned the spots on the heart and bowel again. I interrupted her, "I'm sorry. I have no idea what you are talking about. I thought I was here because I have had some issues with spotting." You could tell she was a bit taken back. She then very professionally and kindly informed me that she would be performing the ultrasound and that a doctor would then discuss the results with me. Needless to say, it was a very quiet thirty-minute procedure. Things moved in slow motion. I felt joy as I saw my baby boy on the screen, but also complete confusion as I wondered what in the world was going on. I breathed a prayer: "God, be with my baby boy." I am so thankful my sister was there. I remember thinking, "I'm so glad I'm not alone."

After the procedure was finished and the technician made her exit, Eileen and I were left to wait for the results. I was surprisingly calm – I think it's because I felt lost. I had never been down this road before. What were the implications of these spots? Were they still there? What did it all mean? I was more confused than anything at that moment. I'm sure the technician was filling the doctor in on not just her findings, but on the fact that I had absolutely no idea of why I was there.

Finally, there was a quiet courtesy knock at the door and in walked the doctor. His face was kind and reassuring, his demeanor gentle and his voice compassionate. He began by apologizing for the fact that I was unaware of the reason for my visit, which, incidentally, was not his responsibility. He proceeded to inform me that the echogenic spots that had been found on the heart and the bowel of our baby, combined with my advanced maternal age (I was only 38, which hadn't felt old at all until this moment), can be what they call "soft markers"[1] for Down syndrome.

Down syndrome.

This was the first time I had heard those words in connection with my own baby. I focused myself and continued to lean in for his words. I was going to have to relay all of this to my husband, who wasn't sitting by my side.

The Doctor continued on…there were no other markers that would indicate a higher chance of Down syndrome. He began speaking of the different options for our game plan. "There are two options here.

---

1 A soft marker is something which may be seen at the time of the 18-22 week scan which may indicate an increased chance for Down syndrome or another chromosome anomaly but which in itself is probably of little or no significance.

First, you can have an amniocentesis, which will answer definitively if your baby has Down syndrome or not. Second option would be that we schedule a Fetal Heart Study, which is an advanced ultrasound of your baby's heart. Forty to sixty percent of all children with Down syndrome are born with a Congenital Heart Defect. This study will let us know if your baby has any heart issues and therefore an increased chance of having Down syndrome."

Although Jer was not with me, I knew what our decision would be. I informed the doctor that I was not interested in having the amniocentesis done. A second trimester amnio carries a slight risk (one in three-hunderd to one in five-hundred) of causing a miscarriage, so I knew this option was out for us. There was no way we would be risking the life of our son for a test. I opted for the Fetal Heart Study, which was scheduled for two weeks later.

Before we left, the Doctor asked if I had any questions. At that moment, I had none. I was a bit dumbfounded at all that had just taken place. He dismissed himself from the room. Eileen and I just sat in silence for a few moments. We both needed to catch our breath and gather our thoughts. We then packed up our items, gave each other the longest sister hug ever and headed for the door.

I think I broke every traffic law as I rushed home that day. As soon as I was in my car by myself, I let it all out. Tears. Weeping. Sobs. What did this mean for the health of my son? What did this mean for our family? I didn't care a lick if the other drivers around me saw me talking to myself and crying like a mad woman.

I was mad. I mean, spitting, cussing mad at my doctor who had let me walk into that appointment to be completely blindsided.

I was scared. What if this is true? What does this even mean? The unknown is scary, because it's just an empty, blank future. You don't know what it looks like—it's like a black hole of nothing, but you know you have to go there. Typically we've painted how things are to be in our lives, and when things like this take place, it takes that pretty, nice painting of our plans we've been working on and just erases it. Empty is scary.

As I approached our house, I began to strategize on how to tell Jer. I knew he was home, because he was running a meeting with some of the leaders from our church. I was in no state to just walk into the house and see a bunch of people. I was a MESS. I pulled into the garage and sent him a text message asking him to come out and meet me. He didn't get the text. Irony at its finest. I never answer his texts when he needs me to! I went to the door and with the calmest, most put together voice I could muster up I said, "Hey babe, can you please come here for a minute?"

I don't remember a lot of what I said as I paced back and forth in our garage, sobbing and telling him all that had just taken place. All of the pent-up emotion from the doctor's office came spewing out and had me on the verge of hyperventilating. I do remember his telling me to take deep breaths and to try and calm down. It was what I needed to hear. He took me in his arms, and we embraced for quite some time. Me weeping. Him quiet. He was now the blindsided one.

We eventually entered the house together. The meeting he was having that day was with some of our closest, dearest friends—the ones we lead Rockford First with. We have been through much together. Even as I write this, I can't help but see how fitting it was that they were all there to receive this news so soon after we had. We quietly gathered together in our living room and prayed for God's peace, wisdom, and grace for this situation. And, most importantly, we prayed for God's hand on our little one.

The two weeks leading up to the fetal heart study were, well, slow. There were lots of conversations with family, prayers, and moments of fear, but all in all, we were fairly calm. When you have two older, very perceptive children living in your home, you can't walk around like an emotional mess! We obviously didn't want to place any unwanted fear in the hearts of the boys, so we went on with life—normal, everyday life. School was just letting out, so the fun of summer and having the boys home all the time helped keep us busy and our minds off of things.

There have been many times in my life when I've learned the art of the "quick toss" prayer. I Peter 5:7 tells us, "Cast all your anxieties on him because he cares for you." The original Greek word for "cast" is *epirhripto*, meaning "to throw upon." The second half of this word, *hripto*, has its own meaning, "to fling with a quick toss" (Strong's Concordance). Often times when we are carrying a burden—a situation, a circumstance, a feeling—we tend to hang on to it and carry it ourselves far longer than we need to. Maybe we feel as though we have to spend quality time with God before we can give Him our burdens. Some of us may even feel we don't have the right to talk with God on our own, that we have to wait until Sunday to bring Him our burdens.

But this word picture gives us a completely different view of prayers—the quick toss. Have you ever played the game "hot potato?" The point of the game is the perfect example of a quick toss. You don't want to be stuck holding the hot potato, so you get it out of your hands as quickly as possible. This is the way the Apostle Peter says we should handle our cares and anxieties. God wants those worries and those cares out of your hands and into His! You can toss Him prayers all day long – whenever, wherever! I literally envision myself throwing Him whatever worry or care I have. The moment fear or worry would burden me, I would quick toss it to God. "God, here you go. I know you have our little one in your hands. I know you have me in your hands. I know the plans you have for each of us are good and full of hope. Amen." Quick toss. You don't need somebody else to do it for you. You don't have to wait until Sunday. You don't have to carry it longer that you have to.

This lesson was such a beautiful encouragement to me as I walked not only through those two weeks of…waiting…waiting…waiting to have the heart study, but also through this entire journey with Paxton. God can't carry our burdens unless we give them to Him. We must learn the art of the "quick toss" prayer!

On Friday, June 17, 2011, Jer and I headed to the hospital for the fetal heart study. After the test, we met with the Doctor and received the amazing news that our baby's heart was just perfect. We breathed a sigh of relief, knowing that this greatly reduced the chances of our child having Down syndrome and all of the accompanying health issues. We were then scheduled for a follow-up ultrasound for early August. We had an amazing summer as a family. Connor had baseball games, we had pool times with family, and finally we enjoyed an extended vacation to our beloved Kauai – all with my growing baby bump.

Honestly, God's peace and grace rested on us that entire summer. So much so that we were pretty sure we had settled on the first name of Paxton for our little one. "Pax" means peace. How truly fitting.

As I entered my last tri-mester, our excitement as a family was tangible. We could hardly wait to hold this little boy in our arms! His big brothers were ready to take on the adventures of the world with him and teach him everything they knew. My due date was October 25, and as the day of our boy's arrival came closer and closer, Jer and I were busy with all of the normal planning and preparing that comes with the addition of a child. Showers were held since it had been a decade since our last baby! I was so blessed by the outpouring of love shared by our family, friends, and church.

On August 8 we headed to our follow up ultrasound. It was another level two ultrasound where they looked very closely for any soft markers, but there were none. In fact, the echogenic spots on the heart and the bowel were completely gone. As the doctor gave us his final thoughts on the findings of the ultrasound, he said these words. "I wouldn't worry at all. Your baby is perfect."

Boy, was he right.

Chapter Five:

Beautiful Boy

*The best and most beautiful things in the
world cannot be seen or even touched—they
must be felt with the heart.*

— *Helen Keller*

As we entered the month of September, the DeWeerdt house was a flurry of activity with the normal preparations you would expect for the arrival of a newborn baby. The nursery was being painted. Teeny-tiny outfits and socks were laundered, neatly folded, and placed in drawers. Our family crib was reassembled for the third DeWeerdt boy. The pathway to our cars in the garage was obstructed by large boxes containing strollers, car seats, a bouncy seat, an exersauser, and the like. Anticipation was building!

My baby bump was no longer a bump, but a full-on pregnant belly. I loved that Caden and Connor were to the age that they would be able to remember this entire experience. They were so excited. They loved to see my stomach move and feel their brother kick as they placed their sweet hands on my belly. There were countless times we sat together, laughing hysterically, as my belly contorted in ways that seemed inhuman. Jer and I knew they were going to be the best big brothers. Protective, loving, gentle, patient and fun.

Sometime in mid-September, I was diagnosed with cholestasis of pregnancy—a condition that impairs the flow of bile from the liver. It causes intense itching, but poses no threat to an expectant mother. For a developing baby, however, cholestasis of pregnancy can be dangerous and most doctors recommend early delivery. Paxton's due date was October 25, but he was scheduled for a C-section delivery on Tuesday, October 18.

As I entered my ninth month, my weekly OB appointments began on Tuesday, September 20. At my following appointment on Tuesday, September 27, I spoke with my doctor about how I felt the baby wasn't moving as much. She immediately hooked me up to the monitors for a non-stress test (NST), which ended with fair results. A non-stress test is a simple procedure in which the baby's heartbeat is monitored, first while the baby is resting, and then while he is moving. Just as our heart beats faster when we are active, the baby's heart rate should go up while he is moving or kicking. His movements weren't bad, but they weren't great either. She also had the in-office ultrasound technician measure my amniotic fluid, which was lower than normal, but not dangerous. My levels were around a nine, and she informed me that if the number ever dropped below five, we would need to take him immediately. Non-stress tests were ordered to accompany my normal weekly appointments, along with an additional weekly NST and ultrasound.

He passed the non-stress tests at my next two appointments, but not without my having to drink a yummy, sugary liquid and the nurse having to use a little tool called a buzzer to wake him up a bit and get him moving. Paxton wasn't passing with flying colors which certainly didn't put my momma heart at ease.

On Thursday, October 6 at 9:15 a.m., I was scheduled for another NST and ultrasound. As I sat in the waiting area for my appointment, the receptionist called me over and said my doctor was on the phone and she wanted to speak with me. This was quite unexpected. They put me on the phone with her, and she told me she had spoken with the doctor of Maternal Fetal Medicine that morning. It was his opinion that if Paxton failed his NST or if my amniotic fluid was any lower than my previous visit, they wanted to deliver him that day or the next at the latest. We ended our conversation, and I headed back to the waiting room. I called Jer on speed dial and told him the news that this baby was probably coming sooner rather than later.

I went back for my NST, which included another sugary drink and the buzzer, multiple times. They walked me over to my ultrasound immediately. The technician tried to make small talk as she worked measuring pockets of fluid. When she was done she dismissed herself from the room. I gathered my belongings and waited nervously for her return. She opened the door and said that my doctor was on the phone and wanted to speak with me. "Jen, Paxton failed the NST, and your amniotic fluid is below five. I want to deliver him today."

"My bags aren't packed or anything. Can I go home to get my stuff, or do I need to go directly to the hospital?"

"I prefer you didn't go home. Our office is connected to the hospital, so we can wheel you over and get you hooked up to monitors."

To say the next few moments were a whirlwind would be an understatement. I called Jer right away and told him the news. They were scheduling the C-section for 5:30 that evening. That gave Jer time to get bags packed, let our families know the plan, and get the boys picked up from school in time for the delivery. Jer is a type-A personality, and he went into go-mode. I just love him. Seriously, no detail is left undone when that guy is around. He even packed my bags perfectly!

I gathered my things from the doctor's office and sat down in a wheelchair for my ride to the hospital. I made small talk with the nurse as she pushed me through the quiet, dimly lit underground tunnel on our way to the mother/baby unit of the hospital. "Alright, Lord, here we go!" I prayed to myself. My mind raced as I was going over all of the details that needed to be taken care of in the next few hours. My heart was peaceful yet excited as I anticipated meeting our sweet Pax.

I got settled in my room around 11:00 a.m. and slipped into something a bit more "comfortable." Beautiful blue gown with a sexy opening in the back—check. Shortly after my wardrobe change, a nurse came in to get me hooked up to the awkward plastic monitors that were secured to my belly by scratchy elastic velcro straps. It was just how I remembered it had been almost ten years earlier.

At this point, besides the nurses coming in for me to sign paperwork and check up on me, I was still by myself—no family, relatives, or friends were there yet. I had a few moments to collect my thoughts, so I took advantage of the time to talk to my Heavenly Father about the unfolding events. Even though this day wasn't going according to script, I had such a peace that all was going to be fine. I knew God was close, so there was a calm confidence in my heart. I took time to breathe deeply, taking in these last moments of holding a child inside myself. Pregnancy is such a miraculous, beautiful experience. And although this was all happening very fast, there was such a sense of relief, because I just wanted this baby here. I didn't want to have to worry any more. This had been an emotional roller-coaster of a pregnancy, and I wanted our child in my arms.

Around 1:00 p.m., Jer and some family members began arriving. Within an hour or so of being hooked up to the monitors, I unexpectedly began having consistent contractions every five minutes. They were beginning to gain intensity; then I had a very painful, very long contraction that lasted three minutes. Everyone was talking and visiting in the background, while I watched Paxton's heart rate dip below seventy for most of the contraction. After the contraction ended, I pushed the nurses call button. She came to my side, and I told her what had happened. She left the room to make a call to the doctor only to return a few minutes later with the news that the surgery had been moved up to 3:30.

This put us into go-mode again. The boys were supposed to be dismissed from school at 3:15, so now we were in a rush to pick them up early so they would make it in time for the birth. We wanted to keep the news of the baby's eminent arrival on the down low because we wanted a bit of privacy as a family before we announced to the rest of the world that our boy was here.

As I was being prepped to go to the operating room, my doctor came in to see how I was doing. We went over some final details, and then the time came for me to be wheeled to the operating room. I said my goodbyes to my family and friends and headed off. There was such an excitement in the room and in all of our hearts! Little did we know the emotional journey we were all about to experience.

Once I was in the OR, I received my epidural and was laid on my back with my arms outstretched. A blue scrim was placed across my chest, obscuring the operating area. Thank you. I have no desire to see all that. At some point during this prep, Jer walked in and was brought over to me. Once the anesthesia was figured out, we were ready to roll. I don't know how you are, but when I'm in these type of moments, I get my game-face on. I turn very serious and focused. I may be smiling on the outside and answering questions calmly, but inside I am all business. I try to mentally stay in the moment and not allow my mind to wander so as not to freak out.

Paxton's actual birth was quite difficult physically for me, although he was only 5 lbs, 14 oz. Childbirth is a big deal under any circumstances, but the medical team seemed to be having an especially difficult time pulling Paxton from the womb. Even though I had received an epidural, I could feel the intense pressure. Pull, push, pull, push. Then there would be a pause, then more pushing and pulling. This went on for about 10-15 minutes. There was definitely a serious tone in the room; no chatter, all business. Despite my best efforts to maintain my game face, I began to cry, and I remember whispering under my breath, "Just get this kid out!" Even though my last C-section birth was almost 13 years earlier, I knew this was not normal. This was way more difficult than it needed to be for such a small child. My strong, focused side was starting to crack and worry was creeping in. I muttered quiet prayers for help under my breath.

Finally, the pressure released, they pulled our sweet boy out of his cozy little womb, and he greeted the world with a tiny little squawk. My boy was saying hello! A sense of relief blanketed the room, settling us all. The tone went from serious to elated celebration! Congratulations and nervous, relieved laughter filled the air. Tears of joy streamed from my eyes as Jer and I shared a kiss. Paxton James DeWeerdt was finally here.

The nursing staff quickly brought Paxton to the prepped warming table where he was surrounded by his pediatrician and the medical team who busily attended to him. As they were cleaning him up, taking vitals, and checking him out, Jer was standing on his tip toes by my left shoulder, excitedly snapping pictures. Getting a clear view was difficult due to all the people surrounding Pax, so he relied on the zoom lens to get close. We so desperately wanted to see our boy. I couldn't see anything from my place on the operating table with the scrim still in place, so I listened intently for every sound Paxton would make. I was listening for the hearty cry I had heard from both of my other sons. The seconds ticked by. He wasn't crying a lot, in fact, he wasn't crying at all. Just quick little squawks every now and then, and this brought concern to my heart. I anxiously waited for each sound he would make, and when the littlest noise would reach my ears, I would exhale a sigh of relief and then begin the waiting again.

Jer recalls seeing the pediatrician turn away from the warming table where he had been attending to Paxton. He made his way quietly over to my doctor and whispered something in her ear. The tenor in the room changed once again. Jer and I both felt it and looked around anxiously. What was going on? Was Paxton in some kind of danger? Was he healthy? Was he breathing well? What is happening? Excitement turned quiet and serious. The small talk between nurses and doctors ceased. My doctor called Jer over to just above my head, over my right shoulder. As they both stood above me, she spoke these words, which will forever be etched in my mind, "I know we had concerns early on in the pregnancy, and it does look like your baby has traces of

Down syndrome." Jer calmly said, "Okay," and then made his way over to my left side and sat down beside me. We sat quietly for a moment, and although I was groggy, I was now tuned in and my senses were wide awake. "Did I hear her right?" I asked. "Yes." He replied, and we both began to cry. What did this mean for the life of our little boy?

Once Paxton was all cleaned up and swaddled, they brought him over to me. I will never forget the powerful urge I had to wrap my arms around him, to touch his face and let him know in a physical, tangible way I was here. But my arms were still strapped down, so I couldn't. With Jer looking on, the nurse placed Paxton next to me, so that we were cheek to cheek, and I remember whispering to him. "It's your momma, Pax. We love you." I kept trying to pull my face away so I could see him, but the nurse would only move him closer to me. Looking back, Jer and I both think this was intentional on the nurse's part, not just to keep us close, but perhaps to keep me from getting a really clear look at him. I have since looked at the pictures Jer took while standing on his tiptoes right after the birth, and, of course, Paxton was adorable, because all DeWeerdt boys are! But he was also very swollen and the facial features of Down syndrome were very pronounced. Maybe the nurse was kindly trying to protect me. I'll never know.

It was time for Paxton to be moved to the nursery. Jer looked at me, and I could see the conflict written on his face. Should he stay with me, or go with our son? "You need to go with him, babe." I said to him reassuringly. I wanted Pax to have at least one of his parents with him as the whirlwind of the first hours of his life unfolded. And so began some of the loneliest hours Jer or I have ever walked through. Jer left with Pax and was faced with a huge decision. Just a few steps away were two sets of swinging doors which led to a hallway full of family and friends, along with Caden and Connor. As I said before, Paxton had the definitive facial features of Down syndrome, so when the adults saw him, it would be obvious. Jer needed to inform them quietly so there was no question or discussion, because he did not want the boys to sense any fear or sadness. They were so excited, and Jer knew he needed to help set the tone while still letting everyone know discreetly.

In a split-second decision, he walked quickly ahead of Pax and greeted everyone with a brief embrace as he whispered quietly in each ear, "He has Down syndrome."

There were a few tears and hugs after Jer went around, but everyone continued to stay collected. Paxton was greeted with deep love and joy, especially by his two older brothers; they could not have been more thrilled! To this day Caden and Connor are Paxton's biggest fans. Jer walked beside Paxton as he was wheeled back to the nursery area where he was weighed, had his footprints taken, and his vitals checked again. Jer recalls seeing all of our family and friends peering through the glass windows, observing Paxton. He said it was such a surreal moment to see everyone's different facial expressions, their feelings on display. Concern, love, questions, somberness, surprise—everyone wondering what this all meant. All the while Jer stood by Paxton, attending to his boy watchfully.

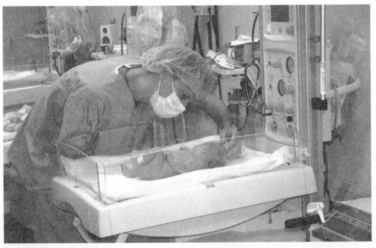

Jer & Pax

I love my husband—such a strong leader, husband, father, son, and friend. I can't imagine the weight he felt in those moments. I am forever grateful for his strength and wisdom during this journey. It was a few weeks later when I learned that after about an hour of attending to Pax, Jer said he could feel his strength about to give way. He asked my sister where there was a bathroom. He made his way down a long hallway to a quiet single bathroom, shut the door, fell to the ground and sobbed by himself for a good ten minutes. He then stood up, wiped his face, and exited. I love his heart.

While Jer had been attending to Pax in the nursery, I was still in the OR getting sown up. This was hands-down the loneliest time of my life. I sobbed out loud like never before. I didn't care who heard me. I didn't care who was in the room. I didn't care that the doctor was trying to stitch me up as my body shook from weeping. I didn't care that I couldn't wipe my own tears or snot away. There was such a heaviness in my heart. I don't know how to describe it. I just know that it ached, and I couldn't hold in my emotions. What was happening? Am I cut out for this? This wasn't in the plans. Great fear engulfed me. What does this mean for Caden and Connor? Our future was now very unsure. My heart ached for Paxton most of all. In all of my confusion, I wondered, what did this mean for him? What would his life look like? What will he have to go through? I've heard it said, "when you have children your heart now walks outside your body" (Elizabeth Stone). I knew this to be true with my older boys, but I instantly felt this at an entirely greater level. Paxton would be more vulnerable, and I didn't know what that would look like or if I could do anything about it.

I knew one of my attending nurses fairly well, and she was the one who wiped my tears and my runny nose with a gentle caring hand. The staff was quiet and worked attentively. When the procedure was done and the blue scrim taken down, my doctor gently hugged me. I often wonder what the staff was thinking through it all. What they were feeling. This I do know: There was no coincidence who was in the operating room that day. The doctor that assisted knew of us and was a follower of Christ. My doctor, whom I had switched to mid-pregnancy, was the perfect presence of calm and grace in a very tense and sensitive moment. Even though I didn't know what was about to go down in that hospital room on October 6, 2011, God knew and had everyone in place.

This was my beautiful Boy, and I was his momma.

I was wheeled to recovery where I was monitored and began waiting for the anesthesia to wear off so I could see and hold my baby boy. I laid my head down and closed my eyes to rest my weary body, but my heart and mind were spinning, trying to process everything that had just taken place. Jer came in, and we were finally able to see each other alone. We sat together quietly, cried together, and then talked about how we were going to be okay. This was our son. Yes, we had a new normal, and there were a lot of uncertainties, but God was not absent and this was not a surprise to Him. Paxton was doing extremely well. He was strong and healthy, and for this we were so grateful.

Eventually my mom and sister came in to see me. Eileen beamed, "Jen, he's beautiful." I needed to hear that. I hadn't seen him yet—I hadn't looked into his face, seen his hair color, or marveled at his fingers and toes. We cried, celebrated, laughed, and had moments of quiet. The emotional side of this entire experience is something that confounds me. There was such joy because this was a life—a beautiful, amazing, tiny, sweet, life! Then there was grief, fear, excitement, sadness, deep love, and you just didn't know what you were going to feel next. My sister had pulled some strings with the nurses, and they had arranged for me to have a room all to myself in a quiet section of the unit. This would prove to be a most treasured gift as the next few days would hold moments that needed a place of quiet and solitude.

Finally the moment came when the anesthesia had worn off enough for me to see my boy. My heart fluttered and beat nervously as I anticipated his arrival. I could hear the cart rolling down the hallway, then the doors open to the quiet, dimly lit recovery room. The nurse made sure he was swaddled perfectly, and then she placed him gently in my arms, right where he belonged. "Hello, my beautiful boy. It's your momma." My voice caught as I said these words; I recalled the appointment months ago where the doctor had pronounced that our baby was perfect. How right he had been. I held my perfectly bundled boy upright on my lap as I traced my finger over his hairline, down his cheek and around his chin. He was sleeping peacefully, so I was able to study and take in the beauty of his slanted almond-shaped eyes, his most adorable button nose, and his perfectly creased pink lips. His cheeks were sweet and rosy and surprisingly plump for only being 5 lbs. 14 oz. One of his sweet hands, with his perfect little baby nails, had made its way out of the swaddle and was resting perfectly by his face.

I was in love. This was my beautiful boy, and I was his momma.

Chapter Six:
Wish Away

The purpose of life is not to be happy.
It is to be useful, to be honorable, to
be compassionate, to have it make some
difference that you have lived and lived well.

— *Ralph Waldo Emerson*

The 36 hours after Paxton's birth held some of the darkest moments of my life. Deep love for my son had an unfamiliar, unwelcome companion named grief. They both settled into that sterile hospital room with me. They would take turns sharing the spotlight and speaking their minds. Love was subdued, subtle, and gentle. Grief, on the other hand, could whisper as quietly as a falling tear or explode out of nowhere, demanding my attention and overpowering me with deep sadness, fear, and guilt.

My lowest point came the day after Paxton was born. Jer had left the hospital to go home and spend time with the big boys, but his parents, Jeff and Linda, were there with Pax and me when a woman dressed in scrubs entered the room with a pushcart full of equipment. Paxton was to have his newborn hearing screening, and she was going to perform it in the room. I was sitting up in my bed, Linda was holding Pax in a chair next to me, while Jeff sat across the room. The technician briefly told us what would take place during the procedure and explained this was a pass/fail test, and he would have to receive a one hundred percent to pass. While the test was performed I would be able watch a computer monitor as the number climbed from zero to one hundred percent. The technician placed a small earphone in Paxton's ear and placed a few sensors on his head, hooking them up to wires connected to the machine that would take the readings.

The atmosphere in the room was still pretty lighthearted at this point. I continued to chat with Jeff and Linda as the test began, but I was also keeping a watchful eye on the number that was supposed to climb to one hundred. Ten seconds went by, and then twenty with the number on the screen still sitting at zero. We all got quiet. All three of our eyes locked to the screen as Pax lay calmly sleeping in the arms of his Grandma. As the seconds wore on and the number remained at zero, there was a sorrow and fear welling in my gut. I was fighting with everything in me to not completely lose it. The test ended with the number still sitting at a big fat goose egg.

The technician nonchalantly removed the equipment from Paxton and informed me he had failed the test, and it would need to be taken again the next day. The instant those words were spoken, an uncontrollable flood of tears and a strong, guttural force of sorrow came forth like I have never experienced. I honestly didn't know I was capable of such emotion and feeling. Now not only did I have a child with Down syndrome, but I also had a child who couldn't hear. He wouldn't be able to hear my voice? Jer's voice? He wouldn't be able to hear me say "I love you?" How would he communicate? I mean, the number never moved from zero. What was happening? I was so grief-stricken I honestly couldn't see straight. I know I was mumbling words, but I don't recall what they were.

My response took the technician off guard, and she quickly packed up her cart and headed for the door. As she exited, two of my good friends, Lisa and Megan, were just walking in. These two, along with Jeff and Linda, can say they witnessed me at my lowest point ever. I had been thrown into deep despair—confronted with a future I honestly could not comprehend, and my reaction was not pretty. Megan and Lisa flanked me on both sides and began to pray as I sat in a heap of brokenness. After a few minutes I began to settle somewhat, and at that moment, my nurse came swiftly into the room. She pulled up a chair beside my bed, looked at me with strong, reassuring eyes and told me how this happens all the time. Some babies need to have two, maybe three tests before they pass, especially babies who are born C-section. Her words were comforting, and as I look back I am so thankful for the insight and care she brought in that moment. However, as I looked over at my dear little boy, I was still very unsettled, and I couldn't help but wonder if that test was correct. Had he been able to hear anything I'd been whispering in his sweet little ears? The thought of it left me undone.

When I finally pulled myself together to the point where I could talk, I made a phone call to Jer and let him know what had happened. The concern was evident in his voice, but he has never been one to get caught up in the emotion of everything. He is calm, even-keeled, and level-headed, yet tender and aware. Shortly after we talked, he sent out an email to family and close friends explaining what had happened and asking them to pray for Paxton. Our focused prayers would be simple— that Pax would be able to hear and that he would pass his test the next day. He gave everyone this verse to pray in Proverbs 20:12, "Ears that hear and eyes that see, the Lord has made them both."

That Friday afternoon after school was out, Caden and Connor came up to the hospital to visit with us. Jer and I had purposefully planned to share the news about Paxton having Down syndrome this afternoon before someone else had the chance to say the words in front of them. Paxton was sleeping sweetly in his hospital bassinet nearby as we circled up the boys to have our family talk. I'm not going to lie, trying to find the right words to tell our boys was not easy. Not to mention we were still in a very emotional state and every time the words "Down syndrome" would come out of our mouths, tears would come to our eyes. "Boys, there is something we want to share with you about Baby Pax." Quiet pause. It was obvious the boys had picked up on the emotions of the moment. "He has a condition called Down syndrome." Connor immediately leaned in and with deep worry evident in his voice asked, "Is he going to die?" Oh my goodness, that was not what we were expecting. What a moment of perspective that question brought. "No! No, your brother is not going to die!" We quickly and calmly reassured him Paxton was healthy and strong. A sense of relief settled on Connor as he leaned back in his chair to listen more. Sweet, sweet boys we have. They just have my heart.

Jer explained about Down syndrome and how Paxton has a little extra chromosome that will make learning a bit more difficult. We told them how Paxton's journey through life would look a little different, but that he was going to be an awesome little brother. The boys needed to hear that their role as big brothers wasn't going to change at all. They need to know Paxton still needed them, and we reassured them that was definitely the case. Paxton would walk, run, play and still need them to show him the ropes of boyhood. There would still be bug catching, mud fights, stomping in puddles, belly laughs and sword fights. By the end of our conversation, the tone with the boys was, "Oh, it's just Down syndrome." What a lesson to be learned from our children who were just nine and eleven years old. Paxton was their brother, he was here, and that was all that mattered. We huddled up, and Jer prayed over our family, thanking God for His amazing gift.

Later that evening I found myself alone, holding Pax in the quiet of our hospital room, his little five-pound body swaddled perfectly and nestled closely to my chest as I softly but boldly declared that verse over him: "Ears that hear and eyes that see, the Lord has made them both." Again. "Ears that hear and eyes that see, the Lord has made them both." Over and over and over I spoke those words over him in prayer. Over and over and over Jer did the same. I can't explain it in words, but as we began to stand on God's Word for Pax, there was a shift happening in us. Our loving heavenly Father began to infuse hope, perspective, and peace into our hearts.

When the sun arose on Saturday morning, we found a renewed strength dawned with it. I can only describe it as the grace of God. Period. Jer and I both woke up with an internal fortitude that said, "Bring it on. Yep, this is our new normal and we are going to rock it. This is our boy. This is our life, and we are going to live it well." It was exactly the mindset we needed as we prepared to tell our church congregation of thousands about the birth of our beautiful boy at service the next day. Oh, and by the way, Pax did end up passing his hearing test! I say "by the way" because that is how it was…we were now living in the assurance of God's GOOD plan for our lives, no matter what circumstances that meant we would face. We had decided to lean one hundred percent on God, and His peace and strength was so real and tangible that the results of the hearing test were no longer the determining factor of our well-being.

Our attention now turned to Sunday's announcement. At this point only a handful of people knew that Pax had been born with Down syndrome. We had kept it carefully under wraps until we figured out how exactly we wanted to word our announcement. As we talked and formulated how to best articulate this news to people, one thing was very important to us – that we honor Pax with how this news was shared. Someday he would hear about or, thanks to technology, watch for himself how his daddy told the world of his son, Paxton James.

Saturday night we placed phone calls to our dearest friends around the nation and shared with them about Paxton and how we had been blessed with an amazing little boy who had a little extra chromosome, which made him extra special. These were not emotional, sad conversations, but rather joyful and celebratory – like sharing the news of a baby's birth should be. Even at three days old, this child was changing hearts and perspectives worldwide. I'm so grateful for our friends all around the world who have lovingly supported our journey with Pax, our little world-changer.

Sunday morning came, and even though I was still in the hospital, the plan was for me to be watching via FaceTime as Jer shared the news (thank you, Apple). I have never been more proud of my husband than I was that morning. With excitement, grace, and poise, he shared of how God had blessed us with a third son, and that he had been born with Down syndrome. Jer remembers hearing a quiet gasp as he said those words. He talked of how Paxton was given to us so we could take care of him, and more importantly, so he could take care of us, and it was already happening. Pax was changing us. He spoke about how Pax was his boy, and he was so proud to be his daddy, and we were proud to be his family. He ended with saying that there were to be no condolences, no pity, no "I'm sorrys" for us or for our family. Because Paxton was our good and perfect gift – the kind of gift that the Father above gives, there was nothing, absolutely nothing, to be sorry about. From that moment on, we have never heard one "I'm sorry" from our friends, family or church, and that's the way it should be. If you have ever met Pax, you know there is something special about him. He truly is a gift, and he has changed Jer and I, our boys, our families, our friends, our church, and our community.

We have the power to set the tone when life sends us the unexpected, when things don't go the way we thought, when life goes off-script. And here's a newsflash: Your life will go off-script at some point. Whatever has happened, whatever will happen, YOU have the power to set the tone. You can set a tone of self-pity, hate, revenge, regret, or anger, or you can set a tone of thankfulness, beauty, joy, and purpose.

Therefore thus says the Lord [to Jeremiah]: If you return [and give up this mistaken tone of distrust and despair], then I will give you again a settled place of quiet *and* safety, and you will be My minister; and if you separate the precious from the vile [cleansing your own heart from unworthy and unwarranted suspicions concerning God's faithfulness], you shall be My mouthpiece" Jeremiah 15:19 (AMP).

Read this verse again. Really read the words. This is exactly what has happened to our family as we have journeyed this road with our Pax. As we continue to give up our mistaken tone of distrust and despair, God gives us a settled place of quiet and safety, and then God uses us, our situation, and our unexpected change of plans to bring light and love to our world. When we cleanse our hearts from the unworthy and unwarranted suspicions concerning God's faithfulness to us, our son, and our entire situation, we are able to be His mouthpiece in the most beautiful, humbling way. There is nothing wrong with the journey of emotions we have walked through (and continue to walk through at some points) with the diagnosis of Down syndrome touching our family. But when we choose to not allow doubt, distrust, and despair set the tone, we see a birth of faith and purpose in our hearts.

God continues to use our experiences with Paxton to be a loud proclamation of His love, light, and purposes in this world. A few months after Pax was born, we were introduced to a ministry called Champions Club, which was started at Lakewood Church in Houston, Texas, by our now good friends, Pastor Craig and Samantha Johnson. After their son was diagnosed with Autism Spectrum Disorder in 2005, God began to birth in their hearts a ministry specifically for children with special needs and their families. There are countless families that are unable to attend church because there isn't a place where they know their children with special needs are not just safe, but are being cared for by trained individuals, learning about the love of Jesus in a creative way, and are valued because they are created in God's image. As soon as we heard the heart and vision of Champions Club, we knew this was something we needed to do at Rockford First.

We got to work! We flew to Houston to see Champions Club in person, and in the coming months began the planning and development process with Pastor Craig and his amazing team. When Paxton was just eight months old, we shared the vision of Champions Club with our congregation, and they jumped on board with overwhelming excitement. In five short weeks, the church donated over $100,000 to see the vision come to reality. The next couple of months were a flurry of activity as we saw the vision come to life. On Sunday, October 7, 2012, the weekend of Paxton's first birthday, we opened the doors for the Rockford First Champions Club. What a celebration weekend we had! What a milestone it was. One year before we had sat in our hospital room scared, fearful, and wondering what God was up to. One year later we were walking through a beautiful, well-planned, purposeful space that would be the place where many children and their families would find hope, acceptance, and the love of our Savior.

Our journey with Paxton has had its ups and downs, there is no doubt about that. There are still moments when the reality of Paxton's diagnosis will hit me like a kick to the gut. There are times when I peer into the future and find myself fearful and afraid. There are still moments when I cry. Sometimes hard, big cries that I can't always put words to. Why am I crying? I just am, because life is different than I thought. Those moments are coming less and less often, but they are

Jen & Pax

there. But do you know what? There are way more happy tears than sad tears. There are infinitely more moments that take my breath away because of their beauty, not because of their pain.

Pax has taught me not to wish my circumstances away, but to live in them, and I mean LIVE in them. Live fully, boldly, bravely, and purposefully right where I am, whether it's the ideal situation or not. When I do that, my eyes and heart open up and so do the possibilities.

I have thought to myself many times, "No Pax, No Champions Club." Without Pax, without this crazy curveball called Down syndrome, without this less-than-ideal circumstance, there would be no Champions Club. There wouldn't be the countless families that can now go to church knowing that their child is in a safe, secure environment where they can thrive. Mom, Dad, Grandma, Grandpa…whomever it is, can now attend service and get filled up with all they need to take on the week ahead. There wouldn't be the volunteers in Champions Club who have been deeply affected by these amazing kids and their families. There wouldn't be the awareness that has grown in our entire family and church for individuals with developmental and intellectual disabilities. The list could go on and on. The changes and stories connected to Pax are far too many to tell. His influence is far-reaching. He has touched more lives in his first three years of life than I have in my nearly forty-two years of life.

So, what is your less-than-ideal circumstance? Are you wishing it away? Girls, we all have circumstances that we wish desperately we could change. I'm not condoning that we sit back and just let life happen; in fact, I'm suggesting the exact opposite. I propose a different idea. Let's take our entire lives and live them to the fullest. Can we throw off distrust and despair? Can we stop questioning God's faithfulness and hang on for dear life to the One who will take us on the adventure of a lifetime if we choose to trust Him? Sometimes our greatest purpose can be found in the very thing we thought disqualified us.

At the start of this story I revealed how I felt I had lost my stride upon

Sometimes our greatest purpose can be found in the very thing we thought disqualified us.

finding out I was pregnant, a stride I had just been feeling I was settling into! As this journey with our beautiful son has continued on, I have to tell you that I have gained my stride back, and then some. More than any other time in my life, I feel like I am doing what I was made to do. My Heavenly Father has used the good and perfect gift of my son Paxton to grow an even deeper and more compassionate love in my heart for others. My awareness for the overlooked and ignored has expanded and caused me to act. I see joy and beauty in the small things that maybe I hadn't before. Things which I used to take for granted, I now celebrate and value more deeply. I am stronger. I am more God-confident than ever. Thank you, God, for Paxton James. I didn't lose my stride, I found a better one!

Take a deep breath and find a quiet moment to ask yourself these questions:

What are you wishing away? What part of your life do you think disqualifies you?

God is able to do something amazing in and through your life in this very area!

Chapter Seven: Take the Leap

Your life unfolds in proportion to your courage.

— *Danielle LaPorte*

The first time, bad weather stopped us.

The second time, someone was sick.

The third time, nothing was going to hold us back.

It was Thursday, October 9, 2014. Myself, the rest of Team Brave, and our daring friend Abby, piled into two cars and made the hour-long trek up to Kenosha, Wisconsin. We were about to do something completely irrational and ridiculous—jump out of a perfectly good airplane 10,000 feet above the earth. Our quest to step into our fears had brought us to this day.

Nervous chatter and laughter about our husbands upping our life insurance policies filled the car as we crossed the border into Wisconsin. Time passed quickly as we jokingly shared statistics about how we were more likely to die in the car ride to the jump site than by actually leaping out of an airplane. Did you know that only one in eight-million skydiving jumps ends in fatality? The odds were strongly in our favor. This somehow brought a great deal of comfort as we headed off on our grand adventure.

Early in the afternoon, we arrived at the small Kenosha Airport. As we pulled up to the industrial looking building, silence settled over the car as the reality of our situation set in. We were actually doing this!! We piled out of the car and made our way to the The World Sky Diving Company, which occupied a small corner office within the main airport building. We crowded into the office to begin our paperwork; I was about to place my life and well-being in the hands of strangers! Qualified strangers, but strangers nonetheless! The tension in the room was real, and it was quite humorous to observe everyone's different way of handling the stress of the moment. Lori was calm, but would put a fake, nervous smile on her face when you'd look at her. Trina was quietly petrified. Abby was happy to be there; she was excited about the jump. Liz stayed busy making sure all the details were taken care of. Lisa started asking a bunch of questions including, "How long have you guys been in business?" Oh, this is your first season being open. Wonderful. "Has anyone ever been injured?" Just one person. Good to know. "Has anyone died?" This is when I interrupted her, "Lisa!!! Seriously. Quit asking questions." We were all becoming increasingly nervous with every question asked and answered.

A kind young woman helped us with all of our paperwork and took our Groupon receipts (Yes, we bought our jumps on Groupon. If we were going to die, we were going to die on sale!) We opted for the video package; we decided it was worth it to have our big moment of insanity preserved forever. Next, we were taken to the "waiver room" where we viewed a video which outlined the inherent dangers of jumping out of an airplane and how it can cause severe injury or death. As each worst case scenario was spelled out, we would look around the room at each other, our eyes the size of saucers. It was only after watching this short film that the clipboard with the final waiver was passed out. We each took a deep breath and signed our lives away with the stroke of a pen.

The jumps were running late that day, so we had about an hour to kill, no pun intended. The adrenaline was already flowing, so the emotional let-down of having to wait an extra hour resulted in a group decision to go to a nearby McDonald's for ice cream and fries—it was definitely a comfort food moment! We were still sitting there savoring our last supper when the phone rang. Everyone froze, deer caught in headlights style. It was time. Back to the hangar we went.

Liz and Abby had to head home early, so they were up first. As first timers, we would be doing what is called a tandem jump; we would each be strapped to an experienced instructor who had done this hundreds of times before. Liz and Abby were introduced to their tandem instructors and then began the preparations. The harnesses were placed on snuggly. Goggles and gloves handed out. Instructions repeated, asked about, then repeated again. It's amazing how attentive you are to instructions when your life is on the line. Photos were snapped. Parachutes packed. Out to the runway they went. We watched as they piled into a teeny, tiny airplane and buzzed down the runway for take-off. No turning back now.

The rest of us piled into a van to head out to the jump zone on the shore of Lake Michigan. Once we arrived we began to anxiously scan the sky for a glimpse of the small airplane that was somewhere ten-thousand feet above us. I wish I had a picture of the group of us standing there with our necks cranked back, scanning the sky as if our lives depended on it! To avoid permanent neck damage from looking up, we eventually lay down on the ground so we could have the best view of the sky. We finally spotted the plane. Tension mounted as it circled around for a few moments, and then, there they were—one jumper, two jumpers. First parachute deployed, second parachute deployed. We squealed with laughter and excitement! Our relief was tangible as we watched them slowly make their way to the ground. We had not, in fact, just witnessed our friends' demise. They had done it! As soon as they landed and were detached from their chutes, we all ran over for a group hug! There was celebration, laughter and smiles all around as we beamed with pride. Oh my goodness, they did it! Oh my goodness, now it was my turn!

We piled into the van to head back to the airport. Trina and I looked at each other. Our time had come. Back at the hangar we went through the same preparations that Liz and Abby had gone through. Emotions were definitely running high. Trina and I have known each other and been good friends for over twenty years. Trina would classify herself as a fearful person overall; one of those fears is of flying, specifically flying in small planes. It seemed to be no consolation that we would soon be jumping out of this particular small plane. I would say out of everyone that was there that day, hers was the biggest leap. We crammed into the small plane, all hooked up to our tandem instructors, and began to buzz down the runway. Trina and I were holding hands; I knew that the very fact that she was in this plane was a huge step. The wheels left the ground, and the hand-holding went to another level. Trina began praying underneath her breath, and I began to pray for Trina under my breath. I looked out the window to take in the view of the distant Chicago skyline to try and get my mind off the fact that we were about to jump out of this plane.

Our instructors turned on their go-pro video cameras and proceeded to try and make light of the situation—what a crazy job to have… jumping out of planes all day with people who were practically scared out of their minds. I bet they have stories to tell! However, right at this minute, Trina and I were not in a joking frame of mind. The best we could do was plaster on our very best fake smiles. There was a definite tension in the plane and you could feel it. As we approached our jump altitude, we received our final instructions and the door was flung open. The cold wind hit my face along with the reality of my circumstances. I am about to jump out of an airplane 10,000 feet in the air, strapped to a man I have never met before today, and I am paying to do this. What am I doing here? Why did I agree to do this? It took a few minutes to circle around to our jump spot, the open door forcing us to look out and down to the itty, bitty world below. I haven't done that much positive, motivating self-talk in a while! "You got this, Jen." "You are not going to die." "People do this all the time." "You are brave." "You are one tough chick." I got the nudge. It was time. Let's do this! 3, 2 ,1…jump!

I have ridden some epic roller coasters, I have gone cliff jumping, I have caught some serious air on our trampoline, but never before in my life have I felt a sensation like that of free falling at one hundred and twenty miles per hour. It was exhilarating. After about thirty seconds of free fall, my parachute deployed and even though we were still falling, the sensation was one of being shot up into the sky—it was amazing. I caught my breath and looked around; we were now floating calmly through the air. I could see for miles. The view was simply stunning; a perspective I had never known before. I let out a loud, excited scream, and began to shout at the top of my lungs, "I DID IT! Oh my gosh, I DID IT! That. Was. Awesome! I'm so proud of myself!" As soon as he could get a word in edgewise, my guide asked me if I wanted an exciting or calm trip down. I figured what the heck—I was already floating through the sky thousands of feet above terra firma, why not live it up! He had me take one of the parachute handles and pull it down to my waist, and we began a fast spin. He then had me release my arm and we were picked up by the air again and brought back to a calm drift. I loved it. Breathing deep the cool, crisp air I took in the beauty as we made the scenic descent to solid ground. My plastered-on fake grin had been replaced by a continuous giant smile. What a ride!

I landed and was greeted with the same hugs that I had delivered to Abby and Liz when they landed. We were losing daylight, so we loaded in the van and quickly made our way back to the airport. Lisa and Lori were the last to jump, and they were the lucky ones who got to see the sunset as they floated through the air. After picking them up (with more hugs and celebration,) we headed back to the hangar to collect our belongings and begin the trek home.

We journeyed back to Rockford with amazing adrenaline highs, memories that would last a life time, and minds swirling with new, valuable life-lessons. The car ride home was filled with excitement as we each shared the details of our experiences that day. Elated phone calls were made to loved ones, and pictures and videos were sent to family and friends. As I drove us all home, I knew that I would definitely be doing this again!

The Leap | Trina, Lori, Lisa, Liz, Abby & Jen

My decision to jump out of a plane was about so much more than having a moment of adventure. It was about marking a new way of thinking and living. Moving past the wishing was requiring me to walk into my fears. Moving past the wishing will require each one of us to put one foot in front of the other on a life-long path that will often lead to places we don't necessarily want to go, places that will require us to face our fears and keep moving forward. This will be an endless climb, a continual challenge to explore summits we used to consider impossible to traverse. The reality is that many times in life in order to have the types of relationships we desire, the careers we dream of, and the influence we hope for, we will need to kick fear in the face and go after it. God's Word is full of His promises and reminders that we will need to be strong and courageous as we live our lives.

In regards to your faith, when was the last time you said to yourself, "Why in the world did I agree to do this?!?" When was the last time you felt nervous, uncomfortable, or anxious about something you stepped out to do? If you haven't asked yourself that question or felt those feelings recently, I would venture to say you have settled a little too comfortably into your Christianity. Ouch. Let's just tell it like it is—Jesus Christ, the one who was beaten, bruised, and crucified on a cross for the sins of the world, isn't super interested in maintaining our comfort levels. When did we start believing that our faith was all about being safe and warm in a womb of tranquility and ease? May we be reminded that the call to be strong, courageous, and brave and the promises that coincide with those virtues are for those who are actually stepping out to do something where those characteristics and promises are needed!

Joshua, a hero whose story is recorded in the Old Testament, was in such a position. God had given him the momentous task of leading a few million people into the land they had been promised generations before. The great news: God was with Joshua! He promised to not fail or abandon him, and that everywhere he would set his foot God would give them the land. The bad news: the land they were to possess was occupied by people who were not friendly, and conflict was imminent. When God gave Joshua this assignment, He also gave him this charge:

> *Be strong and courageous*, because you will lead these people to inherit the land I swore to their ancestors to give them. *Be strong and very courageous*. Be careful to obey all the law my servant Moses gave you; do not turn from it to the right or to the left, that you may be successful wherever you go. Keep this Book of the Law always on your lips; meditate on it day and night, so that you may be careful to do everything written in it. Then you will be prosperous and successful. Have I not commanded you? *Be strong and courageous*. Do not be afraid; do not be discouraged, for the Lord your God will be with you wherever you go. Joshua 1:6-9(emphasis added)

God emphasizes the message to "be strong and courageous" three times in just a short amount of Scripture for a couple of reasons. One, God knew what He was asking Joshua to undertake was daunting; this was not going to be a carefree walk in the park. And two, He knew Joshua was feeling great fear and apprehension. God was not detached and oblivious to Joshua's feelings and the pressure he was most certainly experiencing from the task he was being given, and neither is He inattentive and blind to our circumstances. But just like Joshua, He does expect us to follow through on what He is asking us to do, regardless of how we feel. He didn't give Joshua a way out because he was afraid. God didn't say, "Well, alright, never mind. If you are afraid you don't need to do it." No! Instead God gives Joshua a command, "Have I not commanded you? Be strong and courageous. Do not be afraid; do not be discouraged..." In other words, "Joshua, don't let fear be your guide, let Me do the leading. I am with you every step of the way."

My own personal journey with Christ has been one of continual, consistent, non-glamorous decisions to obediently walk into my fears. Sometimes with tears and a little bit of "Seriously, Lord?" But as I have taken God at his Word, trusted His deep unfailing love for me, and climbed out of the boat, or jumped out of the plane, so to speak, He has been faithful to catch me. He has taken this shy, insecure, fear-afflicted girl and brought her on a journey of trust, which has proven to be the adventure of a lifetime. The first time Jesus ever nudged me to step out of my comfort zone was the early 1990s when I was asked by our youth pastor to greet visitors during our youth service at church. I know it may sound silly, but I remember those feelings of fear and apprehension as if it were yesterday. Back then saying "hi" to someone I didn't know was a huge deal to this reserved Rockford girl, but God was quickly teaching me that it wasn't all about what I wanted or how I felt. My love for God had caused a growing love for people, which in turn became stronger than the fear I felt or the insecurities I carried.

This fear-fighting journey of mine hasn't stopped since then. In 1995 I was asked to speak to a small group of around fifty people. Actually, I wasn't asked, I was told I was going to by my boss, who just so happened to be my husband. I was to teach for an entire hour from the book *Telling Yourself the Truth*. I prepped for days, no exaggeration, and my talk was done in twenty minutes. I'm sure the students enjoyed leaving for lunch some forty minutes early! Lucky for me, turtlenecks were in style back then, so I wasn't completely out of place wearing mine to cover up my bright red, blotchy neck as I spoke!

In 2007, when Jer and I became lead pastors of Rockford First, he asked me to start greeting on stage with him at the beginning of each service. I would sit in the front row every single Sunday before walking up on stage and be seriously sick to my stomach. I kept asking, "Why do you do this to yourself?" Weekly self-pep talks were the norm for me.

Shortly after I started greeting with Jer, he asked me to receive the offering. I would prepare for an hour and have a full page of typed notes for a four minute talk. It took me years, not months, *years*, to become even somewhat comfortable getting up to take an offering or do a greeting by myself. Slowly but surely the edge of fear began to dull. Again, it was my growing love for people, along with an increasing desire to see people grow in their relationship with Christ, that gave me boldness to put one foot in front of the other and continually step into my fears.

Eventually Jer invited me to speak a message with him, then to speak my own message in front of hundreds, then thousands of people. I have to chuckle to myself about how far God has brought me in the sense of leading and teaching. Small steps taken consistently and purposefully lead to great views. The trail may seem to twist and turn and feel like it isn't getting anywhere, but if you simply keep walking in the direction God has pointed you, you will come to places where the spectacular vista of His plan opens up before you. Never underestimate the power of putting one foot in front of the other.

Girls, this is a free bit of truth: surround yourself with people who will push you to do things you don't necessarily think you can do. Don't give voice only to the friends who coddle you and say what you want to hear. Sometimes we can't see the greatness God has placed within us, and we need people around us to help draw that out. I am forever thankful to my husband and so many others who didn't allow me to say "No way!"

We all need to surround ourselves with the kind of people that push and believe and draw out the best in us.

Trusting people, giving forgiveness, being generous, talking to your neighbor, loving those who are different than you, caring for the hurt, eating right, embracing the lonely, sharing Jesus, standing up for the weak, going to the gym, asking for help, walking away, starting, stopping, enduring, helping, talking, living—our fears are as different as our backgrounds, our stories, and our fingerprints. Let's be clear on something, fear is something we ALL deal with. There is not one person exempt from the crippling feelings that can plague us and bid us to stay put, right where we are at. Often we look at other people's lives, and we see where they are at and what they have, and we wish we were there and we had that. Perhaps we think their results came with ease, their obstacles were easier to overcome, or they never encountered feelings of fear, insecurity, and failure. I would argue that in most cases this is completely untrue. I believe it would be safe to say the people you admire and look up to in your spiritual walk must make daily choices to not let fear stand in the way of what God has called them to do. In addition, the Bible is chock-full of people who had to overcome their feelings of fear and inadequacy—and when they did, they experienced a level of intimacy with God and Christ that is only reserved for the gutsy.

Let's take the Apostle Peter for instance. Before he was ever known as one of the mighty leaders of our faith, he was simply a fisherman—a normal, common fisherman whom Jesus invited to follow him. But as we will read below, after Peter's initial "Yes!" to Jesus, he needed some further assurance, and Jesus so graciously provided it. Let's take a look at these two accounts. (Quick side note: Simon is also called Peter, just in case you think I am losing my mind as you read these accounts.)

Meeting one is found in Mark 1:16-18: "One day as Jesus was walking along the shore of the Sea of Galilee, he saw Simon and his brother Andrew throwing a net into the water, for they fished for a living. Jesus called out to them, 'Come, follow me, and I will show you how to fish for people!' And they left their nets at once and followed him" (NLT).

Meeting two also takes place at the sea of Galilee and is found in Luke 5:4-11:

> When he had finished speaking, he [Jesus] said to Simon, "Now go out where it is deeper, and let down your nets to catch some fish." "Master," Simon replied, "we worked hard all last night and didn't catch a thing. But if you say so, I'll let the nets down again." And this time their nets were so full of fish they began to tear! A shout for help brought their partners in the other boat, and soon both boats were filled with fish and on the verge of sinking. When Simon Peter realized what had happened, he fell to his knees before Jesus and said, "Oh, Lord, please leave me—I'm too much of a sinner to be around you." For he was awestruck by the number of fish they had caught, as were the others with him. His partners, James and John, the sons of Zebedee, were also amazed. Jesus replied to Simon, "Don't be afraid! From now on you'll be fishing for people!" And as soon as they landed, they left everything and followed Jesus. (NLT)

In the first account, Jesus invites Peter and his brother Andrew to follow him, and the Scripture says "they left their nets at once and followed him." I picture Peter and Andrew with a response something like, "Woo-hoo! Yes! We are in, Lord! No more stinky, smelly fish for us. This is our chance to do something great with our lives." Well, somewhere between these two accounts, Scripture reveals that although Peter and Andrew were still connected to Jesus, they had obviously gone back to fishing. We are unsure of the reason why, and it might not have been completely negative, but what I do find fascinating is that when Jesus speaks to Peter at the end of the second account, He says, "*Do not be afraid*, from now on you'll be fishing for people." Maybe, just maybe, Peter returned to what was normal and comfortable to him because the commitment Christ was calling him to was overwhelming and fear had crept in. Whatever the reason, this we do know: once Jesus speaks to the very heart of what Peter was experiencing and encourages him to not be afraid, Peter leaves absolutely everything to follow Jesus.

In fact, Peter took Jesus at His word to not be afraid; so much so that he later finds himself doing something downright crazy. The disciples had found themselves in trouble out in the middle of the sea during a storm, and then Jesus showed up walking on the water. The disciples thought he was a ghost, and Scripture recounts in Matthew 14:27-29 (NLT), "But Jesus spoke to them at once. 'Don't be afraid,' he said. 'Take courage. I am here.' Then Peter called to him, 'Lord, if it's really you, tell me to come to you, walking on the water.' 'Yes, come,' Jesus said."

I LOVE this! Have we taken Jesus at His Word to not be afraid, that like Peter we say, "You tell me, and I'll walk on the water?"

Jesus, You tell me, and I'll drop that grudge.
Jesus, You tell me, and I'll become a missionary.
Jesus, You tell me, and I'll talk to that neighbor.
Jesus, You tell me, and I'll ask that person if they want prayer.
Jesus, You tell me, and I'll begin tithing.
Jesus, You tell me, and I'll love the overlooked and ignored.

Just say the word, Jesus.

Often times, we already know what God is asking us to do. We know what Scripture says. We've felt that nudging from the Holy Spirit. We know. So now is the time, dear friends. Jesus says to us, "Don't be afraid." The next move is ours.

Metaphorically speaking, I believe God is calling us to climb out of our boats or jump out of some perfectly good airplanes. He beckons us to step out of the safe and familiar to a place where the views are unlike anything you've ever seen and the exhilaration is unlike anything you've ever felt. He wants us to experience moments where we stand quietly in awe, because we know that we *know* that we *know* God just did something we couldn't do on our own. I'm not saying that life should be one big adrenaline rush with God. But there should be moments where we move past our fears and step out in obedience to do what He has asked us to do. When we give our fears to the Master, be prepared to see how He shows up, uses us, and transforms circumstances and lives.

Jesus
says to us,
"Don't Be
Afraid."

The next move
is ours.

So, why would you jump out of a perfectly good airplane? Why do we need to kick fear in the face and push ourselves out of our comfortable rut? There is a world that desperately needs us to do so. Read on, brave friend, read on.

Before you turn the page, take a few minutes to think about your answers to these questions:

What have you predetermined you can't do?
What have you predetermined you won't do?

There are things in each of our lives that we, in a sense, place a "DO NOT TOUCH" sign over. What are those things for you? God did not create you to live a fearful, "no way," dead-end life! He has great purposes for you; we can take Him at His Word and begin to move past the wishing and into the great adventure this one and only life is meant to be! Here are some promises we can hold onto as we take the leap.

"For God has not given us a spirit of fear and timidity, but of power, love, and self-discipline."
2 Timothy 1:7 (NLT)

"The Lord is my light and my salvation—whom shall I fear? The Lord is the stronghold of my life—of whom shall I be afraid?"
Psalm 27:1 (NIV)

"Be strong. Take courage. Don't be intimidated. Don't give them a second thought because God, your God, is striding ahead of you. He's right there with you. He won't let you down; he won't leave you."
Deuteronomy 31:6 (MSG)

"Haven't I commanded you? Strength! Courage! Don't be timid; don't get discouraged. God, your God, is with you every step you take."
Joshua 1:9 (MSG)

"When I am afraid, I put my trust in you. In God, whose word I praise—in God I trust and am not afraid. What can mere mortals do to me?"
Psalm 56:3-4 (NIV)

"I pulled you in from all over the world, called you in from every dark corner of the earth, telling you, 'You're my servant, serving on my side. I've picked you. I haven't dropped you.' Don't panic. I'm with you. There's no need to fear for I'm your God. I'll give you strength. I'll help you. I'll hold you steady, keep a firm grip on you."
Isaiah 41:9-10 (MSG)

"Since God assured us, 'I'll never let you down, never walk off and leave you,' we can boldly quote, God is there, ready to help; I'm fearless no matter what. Who or what can get to me?"
Hebrews 13:5b-6 (MSG)

"Don't be afraid, I've redeemed you. I've called your name. You're mine. When you're in over your head, I'll be there with you. When you're in rough waters, you will not go down. When you're between a rock and a hard place, it won't be a dead end—Because I am God, your personal God, The Holy of Israel, your Savior."
Isaiah 43:1b-3 (MSG)

"God met me more than halfway, he freed me from my anxious fears."
Psalm 34:4 (MSG)

"Do not be anxious about anything, but in every situation, by prayer and petition, with thanksgiving, present your requests to God. And the peace of God, which transcends all understanding, will guard your hearts and your minds in Christ Jesus."
Philippians 4:6-7 (NIV)

Chapter Eight:
The Half That Wasn't

My child, listen to me and do as I say, and you will have a long good life.
I will teach you wisdom's way and lead you in straight paths.
When you walk, you won't be held back: when you run you won't stumble.

— *Proverbs 4: 10-12 (NLT)*

Why Team Brave decided to undertake running a half marathon together, I will never know. We obviously didn't know what we were getting ourselves into, and it must have slipped my mind that I was forty-one years old, had given birth to three children, had a busy life, and hadn't been exercising consistently for, umm, ever! 13.1 miles is a very long way to run. Very long. Most people can get up and run a few miles with no training (notice I didn't say with no pain), but a half marathon isn't that kind of race. It takes months of consistent training, a major time commitment, and changes to your diet. Not to mention the toll it can take on your body—between all of us we experienced major joint pains, breathing issues, and what runners call "Black Toe." One of us even lost a couple of toenails, I won't say who! Needless to say, as we set out to train for and run the half, we made memories that we will never forget, and ran, as well as laughed, until our sides hurt.

Our race was to be held in Milwaukee, Wisconsin, on Saturday, September 20, 2014, so most of us began training in the month of June. Depending on our personalized running plans, we would run shorter distances 2-3 times a week and then our "long runs" would be on Saturdays, since our race was scheduled for a Saturday. As Team Brave, we strapped on our running shoes, put on our cute running clothes—because that's what girls do—and began the long road that is training for the half.

If you have ever done any running at all, even down the block, you will relate to my next statement: Running can be really, really, really hard! And it was no different for us. Now I know some of you are part gazelle and running comes naturally to you, but the rest of us have to memorize mantras like:

"Your legs are not giving out. Your head is giving up. Keep going."

And that is the great thing about running, or about anything that pushes the boundaries of what you thought you could do. How many areas of our lives have we hung "I can't" or "I won't" signs over, turned off the lights, locked the doors, and walked away from? But if we will unlock the doors and walk through, there is much to be gained. Each member of Team Brave learned so much about herself as we ran. We found we could do hard things such as push through pain, respond correctly to setbacks and failures, and go beyond what we thought we were capable of. The individual lessons gained while training and running were as diverse as each of us, but we were all learning about life and the race we have been called to run as followers of Christ.

I do not like to run. I don't see the point of just—*running*. I have always been more interested in playing a sport such as basketball, soccer, or field hockey. I know these sports involve running, but it is different! It is running with a purpose—chasing a ball, scoring a point, defending a goal. Knowing this to be true about myself, I knew running for 13.1 miles—just to run…no balls, no goals, no defenders—was going to be a challenge for me, but I did have the fact that I am highly competitive working in my favor. I started training at the beginning of July, the hottest month of the year. At first I could barely run two miles. I would have to verbally, out loud, tell myself to not stop running. Other times I would stop, and then physically push myself to start again. I am sure that anyone who saw the vibrant red color of my face thought that something was drastically wrong with me. I remember thinking at the beginning, during my shorter weekday runs, there was no possible way I would make it through my longer weekend runs. As I ran, I would be dreading the run that was days ahead of me!

I quickly learned that past the wishing people learn simply to finish today's run well. I will tell you the same things I learned to tell myself: Quit looking ahead. Stop getting ahead of yourself. You have all the grace, strength and mercy you need for today. Lamentations 3:22-23 says, "The faithful love of the Lord never ends! His mercies never cease. Great is his faithfulness; his mercies begin afresh each morning" (NLT). Such wonderful news! Every morning you receive a whole new unending supply of what it is you need to run your race today.

This truth had been spoken to me years earlier while I was still in the hospital after having Pax. One of the beautiful nurses who cared for us shared part of her story and gave me some valuable wisdom that has stayed with me. In a vulnerable, nurturing voice, she revealed how her grandson has autism and that the greatest piece of advice she could give was to just take one day at a time. I remember thinking, "This is exactly what I needed to hear." She probably knew I was getting too far ahead of myself, and she was right. I was taking myself on extremely emotional time warps into Paxton's future, and it brought me to a dark place: Will people make fun of him? Will he be able to read? Will he graduate from high school? Will he ever live on his own? Will he be able to get married? And the scenario that haunted me the most: What happens to him when Jer and I are gone?

Past the
Wishing people
learn, simply to
finish today's
run well.

I call this kind of thinking "going *there*." There are a few problems with "going *there*." One, I have no idea what "there" really looks like, so I am wasting valuable emotional energy on things I have absolutely no control over. God's mercies are for today, not for my made-up future. Two, when I go "there," wherever that is, I'm not *here*. I am missing out on today and all that it holds. I am robbing my husband, children, friends, and community of what they need, as well as stealing today from myself. Don't get me wrong, it's okay to go "there" sometimes, but let's not stay there. Sometimes I need to face my unknown future, have a darn good cry, eat some cookies and then come back to my now, because *now* is where life is happening. Let's run *today's* race well, with the passion, gusto, and focus it deserves.

As my training progressed, I decided to make my race goal to run ten-minute miles or better, hopefully crossing the finish line in just over two hours. As I trained, I was keeping this pace, and even bettering my times as the weeks went on. I remember the absolute elation I felt when I finished running five miles in just under fifty-one minutes. A couple weeks later I ran six and half miles in one hour and four minutes. I was going to be able to do this! If I kept up my current pace, I would nail my finish time.

That's when things started to go downhill. The first time I ran seven miles, I experienced what felt like a slight tightening of my chest for about a day afterwards. The next time I ran a similar distance, I experienced the same feeling in my chest, but now it was accompanied with some difficulty breathing normally for the next two days. I reluctantly scheduled an appointment with a doctor to see what was up.

My initial visit was on Tuesday, September 9, just under two weeks before the race. The doctor checked me out, and after hearing my symptoms told me I needed to stop running until we got to the bottom of the issue. The next week and a half included a trip to the cardiologist, chest x-rays, and breathing tests, among other things. After all of the tests, I had a follow-up visit with my doctor, and the conclusion was— there was no conclusion. I had now missed my final days of training, and the race was just days away. I was in a conundrum—to run or not to run—that was the question.

The Friday afternoon before the race, we loaded up my SUV and headed to the great state of Wisconsin. I had packed everything for the race even though I had yet to decide if I was actually going to run. As we made the drive, arrived at our hotel, grabbed some dinner, and then settled in for the night, my mind was preoccupied. What should I do? I wanted to run, but I also didn't want to take any foolish risks with my health. Fears regarding the breathing issues I had encountered were weighing on me. Was it even wise to run? What if something serious happened during the race? We still didn't know why I was having the problems I was having, and now I was going to run my longest distance ever after missing the last two weeks of training. Maybe I could go ahead and run and just take it slow, using the approach of walk one, run one. In that case, I could finish, but the competitive side of me knew I wouldn't be able to accomplish the race time I had desired. I laid my head on the pillow to rest for the night, still unsure of my decision.

The sound of our alarm clocks signaled race day was here with the best possible forecast for running—cool and cloudy. It was early, and the girls of Team Brave are not morning people, so we all got ready and made our preparations with few words. I got dressed, laced on my shoes, and gathered my items, still not knowing my decision. Looking back, I think I knew what would be the wise thing to do, but I didn't want to face the disappointment, so I was putting it off. We grabbed our race snacks and headed to the Milwaukee Brewer's Stadium where the race was to take place. The car ride was filled with conversations about last minute race preparations as I quietly navigated our way to the starting line. As we approached the stadium, I tearfully let everyone know I wouldn't be racing. I was heartbroken. All the training, all the determination, all the times I had pushed myself to do something I didn't think I could, all the time invested, all the sacrifice—all with this one day in mind, the finish line, and now I couldn't run the race I had planned on.

The race area was abuzz with hundreds of people excitedly pinning their numbers on their shirts, snapping selfies with their co-runners, stretching, and getting ready to go. We were doing the same. There was excitement and anticipation in the atmosphere. I walked the girls to their starting zone and said goodbye with a hug and a high five. At this moment I had a choice. I had to decide what kind of party I was going to throw. I could either throw a pity party for myself or choose to throw a party for my amazing friends that were actually getting to run the race they had been training months for.

The Half | Jen, Lisa, Trina, Abby & Liz

Can I be honest? It wasn't easy. As I stood on the sidelines cheering them on, I had to fight the urge to play the comparison game. "Why me? I trained too! This was on MY list!" But honestly, what benefit would entertaining these thoughts bring? Certainly none to my life or to my friends I was supporting. The truth is, even though I didn't physically run my half marathon that day, I decided to run one emotionally. I decided to put on my game face and run MY race well that day. I made the decision to push through how I felt.

And it was so worth it. What took place at the finish line reinforced this. If I would have given in to my feelings and emotions that day, I would've been pouting as the other Team Brave members finished their race. Instead, I was their BIGGEST FAN! You know what, if you can't do something, the next best thing is to cheer on someone who can. As they came across that line, tears of joy were streaming down my face, rather than tears of jealousy or resentment or frustration. It was a victory for us all. I conquered the ugly that wanted to emerge that day when faced with a less-than-ideal situation, and the rest of the girls finished their half. We all ran well the race set out before us that day.

I love the beautiful analogy comparing our Christian faith to running a race found in the book of Hebrews:

> Therefore, since we are surrounded by such a great cloud of witnesses, let us throw off everything that hinders and the sin that so easily entangles. And let us run with perseverance the race marked out for us, fixing our eyes on Jesus, the pioneer and perfecter of faith. For the joy set before him he endured the cross, scorning its shame, and sat down at the right hand of the throne of God. Consider him who endured such opposition from sinners, so that you will not grow weary and lose heart.
> Hebrews 12:1-3

This Scripture is packed with truth that challenges us. As we journey past the wishing, yes, we are to throw off the stuff and the sin that weighs us down. Yes, we need to run with perseverance, fixing our eyes on Jesus. Yes, we are to consider all He endured so we don't grow weary and lose heart—because that can happen. All of these things are true and good and important, but what I want to focus on in this chapter is running the race marked out for *us*, meaning the personal race that is before us individually. We all have our own race to run. And although we are surrounded by the "great cloud of witnesses" who are either watching us from the grandstands of heaven or running alongside us, we must run our OWN race. This is your time, your race. No one can run it but you. You will be tempted to quit. You will be tempted to listen to what the crowd tells you to do. You will be tempted to speed up your pace to keep up with others so you can look good. You will be tempted to slow your pace because you don't want to be a show off.

In this life we will be faced with a constant, daily choice to either run the race marked out for *us* or interrupt our pace to play the comparison game. When we run, we are moving and pushing forward, we are gaining ground and making distance. But when we play the comparison game, we are running in circles, chasing shadows, and wearing ourselves out with no real gain being made. Instead of looking ahead and running our race, we become distracted by what other people are doing, how they are running, what kind of shoes they have, what kind of outfit they're wearing, where they are going—all the while our pace is slowing and we are getting drawn into the game. We've all been there, done that.

I have discovered in my own life I can jump in to play the comparison game for two reasons. The first reason is to confirm the insecurity I may already be feeling about who I am and what I have. Everywhere I look, someone else seems to be doing and being more than me—her life is better, her clothes are cuter, she is happier, her car is cooler, she is prettier, her kids are better behaved, she is richer, her husband is hotter, her hair is better, her house is cleaner, she has it all together. Second, I can jump into the game when I need to stroke my ego and make myself feel better about who I am and what I have. I start looking around and thinking to myself my life is better, my clothes are cuter, I am happier, my car is cooler, I am prettier, my kids are better behaved, I am richer, my husband is hotter, my hair is better, my house is cleaner, I have it all together.

Comparison is a great battle for us as women; this is a struggle that goes all the way back to the beginning. We only have to get a few pages into the Bible and there it is—the first woman ever created is playing the comparison game. Let's take a look. Genesis 2:8-9 says, "Now the LORD God had planted a garden in the east, in Eden; and there he put the man he had formed. And the LORD God made all kinds of trees grow out of the ground—*trees that were pleasing to the eye and good for food*. In the middle of the garden were the tree of life and the tree of the knowledge of good and evil." A few verses later we see that God creates and places Adam in the Garden of Eden, giving him the assignment to work in and care for this beautiful place. God told Adam he was free to eat from any tree in the Garden, with one exception. He was not to eat from the tree of the knowledge of good and evil, because doing so would lead to death.

God then sees that it is not good for man to be alone; enter Eve. Eve jumps right into her new domestic role and enjoys helping Adam work in the Garden of Eden. Life is complete; in fact, in the words of God, it was good. The Garden was a perfect place, and Eve had everything she needed. She also had all of the same rights and instructions as Adam; she could eat from of all the trees except the tree of the knowledge of good and evil, or she would die. Well, one perfect day, Eve is out in the Garden taking a stroll, and a serpent came and spoke to Eve. In Genesis 3:1, the serpent asks Eve, "Did God really say, 'You must not eat from any tree in the garden'?" Imagine that, the enemy of our soul planting doubt as his first act of deception towards humans…his game plan hasn't changed much over the years, has it? He still seeks to plant doubt and confusion into our hearts.

The account continues in Genesis 3:2-5: "The woman said to the serpent, 'We may eat fruit from the trees in the garden, but God did say, 'You must not eat fruit from the tree that is in the middle of the garden, and you must not touch it, or you will die.' 'You will not certainly die,' the serpent said to the woman. 'For God knows that when you eat from it your eyes will be opened, and you will be like God, knowing good and evil.'" The enemy was twisting the truth and selling Eve a lie, and unfortunately for all of us, she took it hook, line, and sinker, and now we are invited to be the spectators at the first Comparison Game.

We see Eve's response to the trickery of the serpent in Genesis 3:6, "Then the woman saw that the fruit of the *tree was good for food and pleasing to the eye, and also desirable for gaining wisdom,* she took some and ate it." Wait just a second, we have seen a portion of this response in an earlier verse in Genesis 2:9, "And the LORD God made all kinds of trees grow out of the ground—*trees that were pleasing to the eye and good for food."* Our poor girlfriend Eve didn't have another woman to be comparing herself to, so she started comparing trees! I can just see her quietly contemplating… "So, these trees that I *can* have, they are pleasing to the eye and good for food, but this tree here," as she steps around eyeing it closely, "this one tree I *can't* have, well, it is pleasing to the eye and good for food, AND also desirable for gaining wisdom." The second tree was "better." And that, my friends, is how the game is played.

Eve's troubles began when she started looking around. The beginning of Genesis 3:6 says, "Then the woman saw that the fruit of the tree…" One whisper of doubt from the serpent, and what does Eve do? She starts looking around. She gets out her checklist. And when she does, she sees that what she has doesn't quite measure up. This is where the comparison game starts with us as well. We start looking around. We start making checklists. We start noticing what we have and don't have, and all the while our pace has slowed; we are becoming distracted, and are no longer running our race well.

After Eve started looking around, her comparison led to discontent. We can imagine her thought process, "Well, wait a second, these trees and this fruit I get all the time are pleasing to the eye and good for food, but this one tree I don't have, the one I can't have, is ALSO desirable for gaining wisdom. I have been getting ripped off!" Eve started to believe what she had, what she had been given, wasn't good enough. Don't you just wish you could go back and say "NOOOO! Eve! Stop! Don't eat the fruit! You don't need it. Be content with what God has already given you. You have everything you need. God is good and faithful, and He will never rip you off!" While we can't go back and speak this truth to

Eve, *we can speak it to ourselves*. God has given us everything we need to run the race He has marked out for us; let's not allow comparison to lead us down a dead-end path of discontentment. If we find ourselves wanting MORE, the right response is to become a better steward, a better caretaker and value-adder of what we have!

Eve's discontentment eventually led to great, immeasurable loss. I can't begin to describe the great deprivation that Eve experienced by playing her comparison game. God had given Eve everything, and she gave it up. She gave up her calling to do the work God had asked her to do in the Garden. She threw away the perfect intimacy of her relationship with God. She opened the door to great pain that would not only affect her, but also her husband and the children she would eventually give birth to. They all suffered greatly because of her decision. If we are not careful, the trap of comparison will lead to discontentment and ultimately loss. Isn't it true comparison sucks the life out of you? You start to lose sight of who you are and what you were even created to do. You start to lose who you are in the midst of all the comparing. You lose time, energy, sleep, money, and on and on the list could go. It's time for us to stop playing the comparison game and get busy running our own race. The stakes are too high for us to allow the game to continue! I suggest we become quitters. Yep, that's right. I said be a quitter! Let's quit playing the comparison game and get busy running our race.

So how do we quit this addictive, nasty comparison game? The first way to quit the comparison game is to learn to celebrate all God has given us. In other words, be thankful for what you have! If comparison leads to discontentment, then thankfulness leads to contentment. When you feel the urge to start playing the comparison game, turn down the offer, stop looking around, and focus all you have on being thankful to God for it ALL. Look at what the Apostle Paul says in Romans 1:21 about the power of being thankful: "For although they knew God, they neither glorified him as God nor gave thanks to him, but their thinking became futile and their foolish hearts were darkened." *Thankfulness* is not just a word for the cute plaque that sits in your dining room. It is a powerful force. So powerful, in fact, that when practiced, it will keep our thinking from becoming futile. Comparison is futile thinking; it will get us nowhere fast. But expressing thankfulness to God for what we have places our focus on God, our ultimate coach and pace keeper in this race called life.

When we choose to be thankful, we will experience a surge of energy and strength for the race that is set before us. Comparison will bring your focus onto what you don't have, while thankfulness will shine a bright, undeniable light on what you *do* have. It's that simple. I cannot tell you the life, joy, and strength I have accessed as I have practiced being thankful for even the more challenging parts of my life. Early on after Paxton's birth, I began to thank God for our son every day, multiple times a day. I honestly began to be overwhelmed with gratefulness at the journey we were on. My thoughts quickly shifted from "Why me?" to "I can't believe I get to be this kid's mom!" I Thessalonians 5:16-18 says, "Be cheerful no matter what; pray all the time; thank God no matter what happens. This is the way God wants you who belong to Christ Jesus to live" (MSG). Why? Because God knows that when we take on a cheerful, thankful attitude, it is only a matter of time before we start to see things in a different light.

Another way I have found to quit the comparison game is by learning to celebrate others around me. This lesson was made clear to me as I stood at the finish line of the half marathon and cheered for my friends. With that in mind, we have to ask ourselves some soul-searching questions: How do you respond when someone is better than you at something? Do you shrink back? Begin to feel insecure and perhaps paralyzed? Do you start to distance yourself from her because of how she makes you feel? Do you start to *wish* you had her family, gifts, talents, or life? I have a challenge for you…when you begin to feel those feelings, I want you to do something that will go utterly against what you are feeling! I want you to celebrate what those people have.

Comparison breeds jealousy and envy, and that in turn creates distance between you and fellow runners. They are moving farther ahead, while you are slowing your pace to keep your distance, making your race so much more difficult and unfulfilling than God intends it to be! Why not come alongside, celebrate others, cheering them on and encouraging them in their race? I know this is difficult! *It goes against how we feel and against the very thing we want to do.* But the beautiful thing about celebrating when you feel like comparing is that you both win in the end. And isn't that the point? Besides, the confidence we desire will never be found in playing the comparison game.

And one more question: How do you respond when you are better at something than someone else? Do you leave her in the dust, passing her by with a sense of pride and superiority? Does the fact you are ahead of someone make you feel better about yourself? Well, let's quit that game, too. There's no place for it in the race we are in. The Bible is very clear on the subject of helping those who are in need. Romans 5:1-2 says, "Those of us who are strong and able in the faith need to step in and lend a hand to those who falter, and not just do what is most convenient for us. Strength is for service, not status. Each one of us needs to look after the good of the people around us, asking ourselves, 'How can I help?'" (MSG).

The truth about running this race as we follow Christ is that it's really not about winning the race and crossing the finish line first. It's not about the competition, which is what comparison is. It's not about who is better or who has the fastest time. It's about running your personal best, the race marked out for you. Nothing will give you endurance for your race like cheering for EVERYONE who surrounds you. On the sidelines of the half-marathon that beautiful day in September, I was once again reminded of the beauty of celebrating others. True, I didn't get to finish the race I had planned, but I did finish well the race that was marked out for me that day.

So let's not hesitate to celebrate those who are ahead and those who are behind. I think Galatians 5:25-26 says it best:

> Since this is the kind of life we have chosen, the life of the Spirit, let us make sure that we do not just hold it as an idea in our

heads or a sentiment in our hearts but work out its implications in every detail of our lives. That means we will not compare ourselves with each other as if one of us were better and another worse. We have far more interesting things to do with our lives. Each of us is an original. (MSG)

We have far more interesting things to do with our lives…yes, we do.

As you finish this chapter, take a few minutes to reflect.

Who is ahead of you in the race right now? How can you celebrate them as they run?

Who is behind you in the race right now? How can you encourage them as they run?

Chapter Nine:
Put Your Heart Out There

I'd rather look back at my life and say, "I can't believe I did that"
instead of saying, "I wish I had done that."

— *Anonymous*

During the month leading up to the inaugural meeting of Team Brave, I felt God asking me to step out in some areas that I knew were going to be difficult. As I mentioned before, I felt God tugging at my heart saying, "Jen, I want you to make an intentional attempt to expose your heart to the things that make it ache and just see what I will do." God spoke these words to me as I was driving by the Walter Lawson Children's Home located in the Rockford area. Walter Lawson's is a well-designed residence for non-ambulatory individuals with severe and profound developmental and intellectual disabilities. Living in Rockford my whole life, I had driven by this building hundreds of times, often passing by and wondering about the children who were there. What were they like? Did they have families? How does one end up in a home such as this? Even though I had no idea what took place there, every time I would pass by, there would be a small sting in my heart—a bit of heaviness you could say.

I remember as a small child, questioning my parents when I would see someone who had a disability and was different from me. When I was elementary school age, I was with my mom at a local ice cream shop, and we saw an individual with special needs. I broke down in tears as I asked my mom, "Why?" I have always had a compassionate, sensitive heart for people who were different from me in this way. As I grew up, I thought maybe I wanted to be a special education teacher. In so many ways, I believe God was preparing me for Pax and the future He knew I would have. Looking back, I also can't help but wonder if all along I was supposed to be doing something, anything to connect with some of the people that God had placed on my heart.

As I stop and ponder why I never did anything about what my heart was compassionate for, one word comes to mind: *Fear.* I honestly didn't think I would be able to handle it. I knew to walk into the Children's Home would require a brave heart, and well, I just didn't have one of those. I knew I would be confronted with sights, sounds, and circumstances that would tear me up on the inside. It was going to cost me emotionally to walk in there. And what would I be able to do, anyway? I mean, really? Did I have a solution? Could I really help? What was I to do when I got there? These are the questions that fear asks, and I had been allowing these fearful questions to hold me back.

In essence, the catalyst for this entire book are the words God whispered to my heart on April 24, 2014, as I drove past the Walter Lawson Children's Home—*Jen, make an intentional attempt to expose your heart to the things that make it ache and just see what I will do.* Moving past the wishing will require us to expose our hearts to those things that make it uncomfortable, uneasy, and simply put, dependent upon God. It may be making a phone call to a parent you haven't talked to in years. Or perhaps it's learning about the plight of the impoverished and hungry throughout the world. Maybe it's going to the part of your city that isn't the pretty part, the part you're not comfortable in. Maybe it's trying to love someone you don't understand or agree with. Maybe it's opening up your heart to a child in foster care who needs a family. My prayer is that as you decide to move past the wishing, decide to become uncomfortable, and decide to put your heart out there.

When Team Brave sat down to make our goals, I knew exactly what my first goal would be—visiting the Walter Lawson Children's Home. On June 4, 2014, Liz and I, along with another friend from church, made our first visit to the home. As I made the drive to meet the girls, I was nervous and scared. I prayed quietly that God would give me the strength and whatever else I needed so I could be a blessing to these children. I pulled up, parked my car and hopped out to meet the girls. We greeted each other with a hug and a slightly nervous, "Here we go!" We entered through a side door and met the beautiful shift nurse, Pam. She had planned that we would have a spa day with some of the children, and so we began to help with set up. What happened in the next hour was probably one of the most amazing experiences of my life.

One by one the amazing workers from the home wheeled about eight or so children into a central area of the home where we were to give hand massages and paint fingernails. Although some of their physical circumstances were difficult to see at first, the children all had stunningly beautiful faces. All of them were non-verbal, but many of them would smile as you made eye contact and spoke kind words. Instead of having an emotional breakdown as I had feared, I found God had given me strength to see beyond myself into the hearts of these children. I talked with each of them like we were having a two-way conversation. I told them about my family and what I did for a living. The atmosphere was fun and energetic as music played in the background.

I gave a hand massage to Gabe[1], which he loved. I was able to paint Laura's nails. One of the girls loved to use her voice and made sounds as I sang to her. I prayed quietly over each of them as I massaged their

---

1 Names have been changed

hands and arms. And even though my heart felt a sense of sadness at points, I couldn't help but smile the entire time, and not once was there a tear that came to my eye during our visit. After about an hour, we wrapped up our visit and said goodbye to our new friends.

I had done it! I put my heart out there, and I loved it. Sometimes the things you think will be the most difficult, almost impossible, to step out and do will actually be the things that make you feel fully alive. I don't understand everything about the circumstances these amazing, beautiful individuals are in; we have been back multiple times since our initial visit, and some of those times have been more emotionally challenging than others. We've met a range of individuals from little ones, only two years old, to adults around 30 years of age; all of them with different needs, some being quite difficult to take in. This is what I do know. I have been called to love the overlooked and ignored of this world, and I have a new boldness to do so since visiting my new friends.

Why do we play this life so safe when it comes to loving people? Why are we so afraid to help the hurting? It can be so easy to look at people who are doing great things for God all around the world, in our nation, or in our cities and think, "That is just for them," when in reality God has an amazing love adventure for us if we will just put our hearts out there. Can we push beyond the fear that our hearts will be wrenched and twisted by the stories we'll hear and what we will see? I'm convinced that when we step out, love deeply, and get messy for God, He will give us a supernatural strength to care for what He cares about.

One of the last commands Jesus gave during His time on earth was to look after the overlooked and ignored. Matthew 26:37-40 records, "Then those 'sheep' are going to say, 'Master, what are you talking about? When did we ever see you hungry and feed you, thirsty and give you a drink? And when did we ever see you sick or in prison and come to you?' Then the King will say, 'I'm telling the solemn truth: Whenever you did one of these things to someone overlooked or ignored, that was me—you did it to me'" (MSG). I ended the last chapter with a verse that speaks about the "far more interesting things we have to do with our lives" and caring for the overlooked and ignored will be an enormous part of that! God has a grand adventure of love and purpose He is asking us to step into.

There was a man by the name of Nehemiah who lived a long, long time ago, and his circumstances were different from ours, but his story is one that speaks to what I am talking about. His story is found in the Bible in the book that bears his name. The Old Testament recounts the spiritual journey of God's people, the Israelites, over hundreds and hundreds of years. During this time period, there were seasons when the Israelites followed God, their hearts turned towards Him in love and obedience; but then there were seasons where they turned their hearts and lives away from God. Subsequently, we read stories of times of blessing and then times when things weren't so good. One such time in history is called the Babylonian exile, when a large number of the Jews were forcibly taken from their homeland and brought into captivity through a powerful Babylonian government. The Jewish nation was splintered and their land was forsaken and laid in ruin. Nehemiah now lived in Babylon, but many of his people were returning to their homeland from being in captivity. Let's take a look at his story and see how it speaks to our journey of moving past the wishing.

> These are the memoirs of Nehemiah son of Hacaliah. In late autumn, in the month of Kislev, in the twentieth year of King Artaxerxes' reign, I was at the fortress of Susa. Hanani, one of my brothers, came to visit me with some other men who had just arrived from Judah. I asked them about the Jews who had returned there from captivity and about how things were going in Jerusalem. They said to me, "Things are not going well for those who returned to the province of Judah. They are in great trouble and disgrace. The wall of Jerusalem has been torn down, and the gates have been destroyed by fire." When I heard this, I sat down and wept. In fact, for days I mourned, fasted, and prayed to the God of heaven. (Nehemiah 1:1-4)

Nehemiah's story starts with a question. He was curious about what was going on outside of his own world; outside of where he lived his everyday life, his normal, ride the donkey to work, punch in, punch out, ride the donkey home and do it all again tomorrow life. And that's where it will begin with us. Simply asked, what are you curious about? I was curious about the Walter Lawson Children's Home for YEARS!!!! What have you wondered about? Is it the poor and underprivileged in your city? Is the plight of orphans around the world? Is it the need for clean water in developing nations? Is it the elderly neighbor that lives three doors down? Is it the literacy program in your city? What has piqued your curiosity? Now start asking questions. Start learning, start reading, start talking, start asking. Simply start. Don't make loving people too complicated. I've found that sometimes we don't ask the question, because we are afraid of the answer.

The answer that Nehemiah heard back from his brother about the state of his homeland rocked his world. His people were in great trouble and disgrace, and this brought Nehemiah to his knees with weeping. In fact he mourned, fasted, and prayed to God for days. His heart was broken for his people, and it drove him to his knees in prayer. It didn't drive him to be bitter. It didn't drive him to question if God was good. It didn't drive him to have a hardened heart. It didn't drive him to be angry towards God.

> Then I said, "O Lord, God of heaven, the great and awesome God who keeps his covenant of unfailing love with those who love him and obey his commands, listen to my prayer! Look down and see me praying night and day for your people Israel. I confess that we have sinned against you. Yes, even my own family and I have sinned! We have sinned terribly by not obeying the commands, decrees, and regulations that you gave us through your servant Moses. Please remember what you told your servant Moses: 'If you are unfaithful to me, I will scatter you among the nations. But if you return to me and obey my commands and live by them, then even if you are exiled to the ends of the earth, I will bring you back to the place I have chosen for my name to be honored.' The people you rescued by your great power and strong

hand are your servants. O Lord, please hear my prayer! Listen to the prayers of those of us who delight in honoring you. Please grant me success today by making the king favorable to me. Put it into his heart to be kind to me." (Nehemiah 1:5-11)

Nehemiah's burden drove him to humbly pray for his people, to confess his sins, as well as the sins of his family and his nation, to ask God to remember His promises, and to ask for help in what he was to do next. I can't think of a more beautiful response than the one of Nehemiah. So often, we let the things that hurt our heart harden our heart; but God wants to do a work in our heart if we will bring our burdens to Him. Yes, God is big enough for our questioning, and we all have questions, but maybe, just maybe, if we take Nehemiah's approach, we will see God shift our hearts.

You can tell by the end of Nehemiah's prayer in chapter 1 verse 11 that God is already birthing a rescue plan in him, because he asks for favor to be granted by the king, his boss. Nehemiah worked for the king as a cupbearer. The role of the cupbearer was to take a bite or a sip every time the king wanted to eat or drink something to make sure no one was trying to poison him. I bet when Nehemiah got the position he didn't think, "YES!!! I get to eat gourmet foods and taste the finest wines in the land! Jackpot!" Nehemiah's job wasn't glamorous; he had to put his life on the line for the king every single day, but because Nehemiah served the king faithfully, the king trusted Nehemiah. They spent all day, every day together, and we know they were close because the king noticed Nehemiah's sadness. I can't help but think that Nehemiah was divinely placed exactly where he was, with the relationship he had with the king, in order to help carry out the rescue plan God had placed in his heart. And we are no different. What may have seemed like a bum deal to you—the job you didn't want, the family you didn't sign up for, the diagnosis you didn't have planned—God can and will use the *place* you are at, the *people* you know, and the *position* you are in for His purposes, whether you think it is ideal or not.

Early the following spring, in the month of Nisan, during the twentieth year of King Artaxerxes' reign, I was serving the king his wine. I had never before appeared sad in his presence. So the king asked me, "Why are you looking so sad? You don't look sick to me. You must be deeply troubled." Then I was terrified, but I replied, "Long live the king! How can I not be sad? For the city where my ancestors are buried is in ruins, and the gates have been destroyed by fire." (Nehemiah 2:1-6)

The moment the king asks Nehemiah why he has been so sad comes some time after Nehemiah heard the news about the state of Jerusalem. Nehemiah has been praying and waiting, all the while his heart is breaking. The time finally comes when Nehemiah has his chance to share his heart with the king. The king asks Nehemiah why he is so sad, and Nehemiah knows this is his opportunity to do something. When writing about this moment in his memoir, Nehemiah states, "Then I was terrified, BUT I replied…" I love that he gives us this glimpse into his journey. He was terrified! The King James Version says "Very sore afraid" meaning "vehemently increased fright." (Strong's Concordance) This was the feeling Nehemiah had, BUT he spoke up anyway; he did what he knew he needed to do. Whether or not we are supposed to do something for God has nothing to do with the presence of fear or with how we feel at all; it has everything to do with the burden He has placed on our hearts and what He has called us to do. Nehemiah's burden for his homeland, his nation, and his people caused him to overcome being terrified. May our burden be louder and bolder than our strongest, most terrifying fear.

The king asked, "Well, how can I help you?" With a prayer to the God of heaven, I replied, "If it please the king, and if you are pleased with me, your servant, send me to Judah to rebuild the city where my ancestors are buried." The king, with the queen sitting beside him, asked, "How long will you be gone? When will you return?" After I told him how long I would be gone, the king agreed to my request. I also said to the king, "If it please the king, let me have letters addressed to the governors of the province west of the Euphrates River, instructing them to let me travel safely through their territories on my way to Judah. And please give me a letter addressed to Asaph, the manager of the king's forest, instructing him to give me timber. I will need it to make beams for the gates of the Temple fortress, for the city walls, and for a house for myself." (Nehemiah 2:4-8a)

Nehemiah takes this first step of telling the king his situation and the king asks, "Well, how can I help you?" With a prayer to God of heaven, Nehemiah takes the ball and runs with it. He gains boldness as he continues in his conversation with the king, asking the king for special letters addressed to different government officials so he can get where he needs to go and obtain the supplies he needs to make his job possible. After Nehemiah takes a big gulp and tells the king why he has been so sad, he becomes increasingly emboldened to ask for more! I'm not a Bible scholar, but it sounds as if Nehemiah is getting the king to pay for the timber for the rebuild. I love this! Could it be that once we take that initial step into our big, bad fears, we will begin to gain a God-given boldness to keep asking, to keep going, to keep running? I think so.

And the king granted these requests, because the gracious hand of God was on me. (Nehemiah 2:8b)

Nehemiah was both bold and humble. He was wise enough to know that anything he accomplished was only because the gracious hand of God was on him. I pray that would be said of all of us. As we begin to gain boldness in our walk with the Lord, as He begins to open doors for us, as we begin to do great things with Him, as we begin to get noticed, perhaps, for our work, our attitude and posture would always come back to this one sentence: "And the king granted these requests, because the gracious hand of God was on me." May we be wise enough to know that anything we EVER, EVER, EVER accomplish is because of God's favor and hand upon us. Period.

When I came to the governors of the province west of the Euphrates River, I delivered the king's letters to them. The king,

I should add, had sent along army officers and horsemen to protect me. But when Sanballat the Horonite and Tobiah the Ammonite official heard of my arrival, they were very displeased that someone had come to help the people of Israel. (Nehemiah 2:9-10)

As Nehemiah nears his homeland, he delivers some of his letters to government officials, and word trickles out that he has arrived on the scene to help his people rebuild their city and their walls. Two men in particular, Sanballat and Tobiah, were not happy about this; in fact it says they were "much disturbed that someone had come to promote the welfare of the Israelites." Nehemiah was stirring the waters, he was rocking the boat, and people weren't happy about it. When you begin to put feet to the burden God has placed on your heart, you will disturb people. You may hear one-liners like these: "Why would you do that?" "You don't have time for that." "What difference is that going to make?" "You want to give how much money?" "You want to go where?" "Isn't that a little extreme?" Some people won't understand. Maybe you will be made fun of. You might lose some friends. Some people will try to stop you. Love people anyway. Help people in distress anyway. Remember your burden and continue with the plan God has placed in your heart.

Then Eliashib the high priest and the other priests started to rebuild at the Sheep Gate. They dedicated it and set up its doors, building the wall as far as the Tower of the Hundred, which they dedicated, and the Tower of Hananel. People from the town of Jericho worked next to them, and beyond them was Zaccur son of Imri. The Fish Gate was built by the sons of Hassenaah. They laid the beams, set up its doors, and installed its bolts and bars. Meremoth son of Uriah and grandson of Hakkoz repaired the next section of wall. Beside him were Meshullam son of Berekiah and grandson of Meshezabel, and then Zadok son of Baana. Next were the people from Tekoa, though their leaders refused to work with the construction supervisors. The Old City Gate was repaired by Joiada son of Paseah and Meshullam son of Besodeiah. They laid the beams, set up its doors, and installed its

May our
Burden be
louder and bolder
than our strongest,
most Terrifying
fear.

bolts and bars. Next to them were Melatiah from Gibeon, Jadon from Meronoth, people from Gibeon, and people from Mizpah, the headquarters of the governor of the province west of the Euphrates River. Next was Uzziel son of Harhaiah, a goldsmith by trade, who also worked on the wall. Beyond him was Hananiah, a manufacturer of perfumes. They left out a section of Jerusalem as they built the Broad Wall. (Nehemiah 3:1-8)

You may be wondering why I included these eight verses from chapter three for you to read. Actually the entire chapter is exactly like the first eight verses. It paints a picture of the wall being rebuilt, with different groups of people owning the repairs for certain sections of the wall. I know it's hard for us to understand a culture from thousands of years ago, but believe me, the walls of Jerusalem were in need of serious work. And the job was huge! They didn't have bulldozers, cranes, and dump trucks. They had people, animals, and hand tools. Nehemiah knew it was going to take time to rebuild everything that had been broken, but he was committed to the project, and he also knew a secret. If everyone did their part, if every family or group worked hard on the section assigned to them, the job could be finished.

Sometimes we can get so overwhelmed at the brokenness and hurt in our world that we throw up our hands and call it quits before we even start. There is no denying the job is huge and it may seem impossible. However, I have often thought that if every single person who is a Christ follower actually did the job of repairing the wall in front of them—of actually doing something about what they were curious about, of actually praying for what breaks their heart, and then actually working the plan God placed in their heart—the job of loving and caring for the overlooked and ignored in this world would be so much further along. If we each moved past the wishing and got to work repairing the section of broken wall in front of us, what a difference we could make!

We are more like Nehemiah than we think. Oh my dear friends, it is my prayer that we would not sit back and keep our hearts all comfortable and protected in the safety of our comfort zone. You've heard it all throughout this book, but I am going to say it again: You have this one, beautiful life; how are you going to allow God to use you to love other people? There is a world out there that is broken down, hurt, alone, and vulnerable, and we must get to work on our section of the wall. Jesus commands us as his followers to be his love and the light wherever we may go.

My visit to Walter Lawson Children's Home has become a part of my continuing journey to follow God's leading and expose my heart to the things that make it ache. I've learned to bring my brokenness and burden to my Father God, and then He in turn gives me boldness and a plan to work. He lovingly reminds me He has placed me where I am and given me the talents, gifts, and heart for this time, right here and now. I love that God is ever so patient with me as I learn and grow in His purposes for me. He's not upset or angry that I'm 41 and just learning these lessons; He's glad my heart is open and I'm leaning on Him to help me. I invite you to join me in putting your heart out there! Let's just see what God will do!

Part of moving past the wishing is taking time to reflect and apply.

Who or what are you curious about? What has struck a chord in your heart that you would like to move past the wishing and do something about?

Begin praying the same way Nehemiah did. Remember his burden drove him to humbly pray for his people, to confess his sins, as well as the sins of his family and his nation, to ask God to remember His promises, and to ask for help in what he was to do next.

Listen and get to work!

Chapter Ten:
Girls in Carhartts

Look closely at the present you are building.
It should look like the future you are wishing for.

Have you ever been part of a renovation project? Or perhaps even built a home or some other type of building from the ground up? It is a very painstaking and long process. First comes the idea. Then architectural plans are made, then revised, then reviewed, then revised again… multiple times. Contractors are chosen, supplies are bought, and then more supplies are bought! Money is spent. Work clothes get dirty. Hands get blisters, cuts, and scratches. More money is spent!

About eleven years ago Jer and I finished our basement, taking it from a simple, open concrete space and creating one bedroom, a large rec area, and a full bathroom. For months and months every single minute was taken up with planning, sorting out the details, and just a whole lot of hard work. Every evening after the kids went to bed Jer was building walls and I was staining trim and doors. We cut trim, hung doors, painted walls, and filled nail holes. Contractors were hired to do what we couldn't and then we wrote them checks. It seemed like a never-ending process, but the end product was amazing. We now have a beautiful, roomy space where we make memories and guests are able to come stay. Room and space were added when we took the time to plan and work hard.

And life is no different. As we embark on this journey of moving past the wishing, we find ourselves on a building site, one where we get to be a part of building something beautiful and breathtaking. We are creating room and space where our lives can be lived and others can find a place that gives life. Proverbs 14:1 states, *"A wise woman builds her home, but a foolish woman tears it down with her own hands"* (NLT). Our "homes" are not just our physical homes; but our marriages, families, friendships, our whole lives! When you build a home you get to choose your floor plan—how many bedrooms and bathrooms you have, the color of the walls, the landscaping and light fixtures—and it is the same with building a life. We get to choose. We get to be a part of the decision-making process. So, girls, let's put on our Carhartts, pull on some gloves, and get to work. Let's not be afraid to let the dust fly!

How do we build our lives like Proverbs 14:1 talks about?

We start with first things first by inviting God to be our General Contractor, the one who is ultimately in charge of our build. Moving past the wishing is not about using our will power to change our circumstances, attitudes, and life in general. Yes, we have a part to play, but I want us all to take a big, long deep breath for a moment and remember when we invite God into our lives He is the one who gives us the strength, determination, and wisdom to help us become a wise builder. In a regular home build, the general contractor is the person overseeing the project. They are on-site daily to make sure the job is getting done right. Girls, we must allow God to be this hands-on in our lives. I believe inviting God into our past the wishing journey is the most important step we can take. Allow Him to be in charge. Invite Him daily, hourly into the conversation and the process. Surrender the plans to Him, and rely on His strength. It's so reassuring when we know we are running all our plans through Him.

I want you to take a few minutes to pause and really think about the answers to the questions I'm about to ask you. Don't hurry on to what's next; take some time to pause and maybe even write down some of your thoughts.

What do you envision for your life?
What type of person do you want to be?
What do you want your relationships (friends, family, marriage) to look like?

If you are like me, you are fighting the urge to rush past these questions. Don't. Put this book down and take a walk if you need to. Talk to God about the answers. Let yourself dream a little. This process is important, so don't short change it. We will never know what we are building if we don't take the time to really think about what we want to build. Every single day we are building, so let's begin to be intentional about WHAT we are building towards! Imagine the outcome of a physical build that was done haphazardly, without any foresight or planning. Yikes! All functional, working, beautiful buildings had some sort of an architectural plan that spelled out exactly what was wanted. We need to have a vision of what we want and start working towards it.

Have you ever looked at a set of architectural plans for a home or a building? No small amount of time and intentionality goes into such plans. As we are becoming a wise builder of our one and only life, we will have to make thoughtful plans, and thoughtful plans take TIME. Ah, time, that thing we never have enough of. Yes, that's what making plans will take. Proverbs 22:5 hits the nail on the head when it comes to plans, "Good planning and hard work lead to prosperity, but hasty shortcuts lead to poverty" (NLT). After we take the time to make some well laid out plans, we will always have them to refer back to when we are building. The decisions we make tie back to our plans. The plans will help determine where we go, what we do, and how we live our lives. They will become a map for the journey ahead, and a reminder of where we want to be headed. The plans take the pressure off the daily decisions. Without a plan, each decision is a crisis. With a plan to refer back to, each decision has a pre-set path to follow. What a relief!

It's important to remember that once we've made our plans and have a vision for what we want our lives to be, there will be a cost involved in the building. What kind of cost? Time, energy, effort, money, putting others first, laying down our pride, and foregoing personal comforts are just a few. Whatever you envision will have a corresponding expense. I don't know what that expense will be for you exactly, but before you build, it's important to count the cost. Luke 14:28-30 sums it up perfectly, "Is there anyone here who, planning to build a new house, doesn't first sit down and figure the cost so you'll know if you can complete it? If you only get the foundation laid and then run out of money, you're going to look pretty foolish. Everyone passing by will poke fun at you: 'He started something he couldn't finish'" (MSG). Now, don't take this as a cue to not do what you've envisioned! I'm simply saying that you really need to think and pray through whether or not you are willing to pay for what you want. It's important to know what you are getting yourself into. Although there are always some unforeseen costs in a building project, if you know what you have signed up for, you're less likely to let the small surprises stop you and your progress.

Have you ever tried to undertake a project around your house without the right tools? If you don't have the right tools, a job can last way longer and be way more difficult than it needs to be. This little life-building project we are undertaking is no different. Everything will be more difficult if we don't have the two innovative, life-changing tools: Prayer and the Word of God. Go ahead, skip this paragraph because you've heard it all before, right? Correct. I'm not going to say anything you probably haven't already heard, but I do want to challenge us in these areas. Building the life you want will take longer and be more difficult without the consistent use of these tools. It's just the way it works. I've tried to build without them, and I've tried to build using them, and the latter is the way to go.

I want to call us back to the disciplines of devoted, daily reading of the Bible and passionate, consistent prayer. These tools are what give you connection with Jesus Christ who is the "author and finisher of our faith" (Hebrews 12:2). In fact, Matthew 7:24-27 speaks of how God's Word is foundational for our life:

> These words I speak to you are not incidental additions to your life, homeowner improvements to your standard of living. *They are foundational words, words to build a life on.* If you work these words into your life, you are like a smart carpenter who built his house on solid rock. Rain poured down, the river flooded, a tornado hit—but nothing moved that house. It was fixed to the rock. But if you just use my words in Bible studies and don't work them into your life, you are like a stupid carpenter who built his house on the sandy beach. When a storm rolled in and the waves came up, it collapsed like a house of cards (MSG, *emphasis added*).

So not only is reading the Bible a tool, it will also be a strong foundation on which to build your house. It is that important! Let's fall in love with God's Word all over again, or for the first time. God's Word is a "lamp unto our feet and a light unto our path" (Psalm 119:105). In Psalm 1 we are also told when we meditate on God's Word, we will flourish and prosper like a tree planted by a river. I'll admit, sometimes it can be very easy to neglect the Bible, and before I know it, days and weeks have gone by and I haven't even opened my Bible.

There are many things that can keep us from picking up the Bible— maybe we are intimidated by the "holy book," and we don't even know where to even begin! Maybe we are apathetic and have just forgotten why it's important. If you don't understand the Bible, find a friend or a leader in your church who can help you grow in your understanding. Or another idea is when you and your Team Brave meet up, take time to read a passage of Scripture together and discuss it. Maybe you could do a Bible study together, or read a book together regarding prayer and scripture. Find a version of the Bible that is written in more modern English to help you in your understanding. Many Study Bibles contain notes and commentary which help bring color and insight to what you are reading. There are also amazing daily devotionals, which can help you begin a daily habit by giving you a simple verse and thought for your day. It is my prayer that we would be women who passionately love God's Word, and desire to connect with Jesus in prayer.

Sometimes we make prayer too complicated. In the simplest of terms, prayer is talking to God. God wants to hear from us. We can pray whenever, wherever, about whatever, and He hears us. It doesn't have to be flowery or fancy. In fact it can be simple. In Matthew 6:5-8, Jesus is speaking to His disciples about prayer:

> "The world is full of so-called prayer warriors who are prayer-ignorant. They're full of formulas and programs and advice, peddling techniques for getting what you want from God. Don't fall for that nonsense. This is your Father you are dealing with, and he knows better than you what you need. With a God like this loving you, you can pray very simply" (MSG).

Don't mistake simple as weak! Prayer is powerful, and I want to challenge us to up our game in prayer. Let's keep it simple, but let's DO it! Often times, we forget the power that prayer has. We so often take the situations in our lives at face value rather than bringing them to God in prayer and believing in faith that things can change. Jesus says in Mark 11:22-24:

> "Have faith in God," Jesus answered. "Truly I tell you, if anyone says to this mountain, 'Go, throw yourself into the sea,' and does not doubt in their heart but believes that what they say will happen, it will be done for them. Therefore I tell you, whatever you ask for in prayer, believe that you have received it, and it will be yours."

I want to encourage you to become a student of prayer. Read books about prayer, talk to people who pray and made it a habit. And by all means, pray. Talk to God, all the time. Ask Him to teach you how to pray and begin the practice of prayer. Turn your wishes into prayers.

Building isn't just about laying a strong foundation and putting up quality walls. Sometimes, building involves demolition and renovation! Remember the good and faithful servants I spoke of in chapter one—the ones that added value to what the Master had entrusted to them? Notice that Jesus doesn't call the servants "perfect and never-failing" servants when He commends them. He calls them "good and faithful." On this journey there will be failure, there will be times when you blow it, times when you get it all wrong, times when you build a wall where you shouldn't, and you don't like the landscape you let take root. So guess what...change it. That mistake isn't forever. Let's just be faithful. Let's not leave the building site.

It is important that we never confuse the necessary demolition of building mistakes with the destructive practice I am going to call "tearing down." It is a foolish woman who, in moments of negativity, tears down good things that have been built. There are many ways that we as women can tear down our homes, our lives, but I believe one of the greatest ways is by complaining and whining about our circumstances.

> *My kids drive me crazy.*
> *My husband doesn't do anything.*
> *That one lady at work is so annoying.*
> *That neighbor of mine drives me crazy, and she dresses like a floozy.*
> *I just can't get ahead.*
> *Life is just too hard.*
> *God isn't for me.*
> *He doesn't love me.*
> *That other family has it easier.*
> *Life just is what it is and I can't change it.*

Complaining is the mother tongue of a wisher. The more we do it, the more it flows right out of us. It is imperative for us to realize these attitudes work against the very life we are attempting to build. Complaining will never, ever change our circumstances into what we desire them to be. When you complain, things remain the same; the only thing that really changes is us—and not in a good way! Our outlook becomes tainted with negativity, and we quickly become "the glass is half empty" kind of people.

I did an experiment a couple of years ago with this whole complaining thing. Rockford winters can become long, and I had settled into a mindset of complaining and whining about the weather as soon as Christmas was over. Everyone enjoys a white Christmas with a chill in the air, but after that, I was done. I complained about the snow, the cold, the dirty roads, dirty cars, not being able to go outside, waaaah, waaaah, waaaah. Everyday was an "ugh" day, a "blah" day. I hated winter, and that attitude was affecting my outlook and my attitude. About three winters ago, I decided to stop the whining. I committed to stop complaining out loud AND in my mind about the weather. It was so freeing. Obviously, my complaining about the weather was never going to change the weather. But my grumbling and my negativity were changing me. Both my spirit and heart were heavier, and I was allowing my circumstances to dictate my feelings and emotions. Complaining is easy to do, just like tearing something down is easy to do. Let's commit to stop complaining. For some of us that may actually need to be put on your Team Brave goal list, because your complaining isn't just what you do, it has become who you are. But you are called to build, wise friend. So, let's stop tearing down.

As you're planning, working, and building, things will get messy. When we talk about living this one, amazing life to the fullest, we must be careful not to confuse that sentiment with a false picture of a perfect, blissful, and always calm life. Life is messy; it isn't always clean, and this journey of moving past the wishing won't always be either. Don't lose sight of your plans when the going gets tough. Don't forget who your General Contractor is. Remember you've calculated the cost, and you're

Living a brave, intentional life requires putting on our work pants and boots, grabbing our tools, and getting to Work.

willing to pay the price. Don't forget your tools. They are foundational to your growth.

So I have a question for you. Are you a wisher or a builder? Or maybe a better question is—which do you want to be?

I want to be an intentional builder of my life. Will you join me? I want us to know that living a brave, intentional life isn't all adrenaline and goose bumps. Moving past the wishing and into a brave, intentional life is about daily putting on our work pants, work boots, grabbing our tools and getting to work. God has a grand vision for your life, but His question back to you is, "Do you have a grand vision for your life?" If not, then let's get one! Yes, I know it will take time, effort, sweat, hard work, discipline, courage, investment, and bravery; but you are worth it. Let me say that again, YOU ARE WORTH IT! And so are your kids, spouse, friends, church, and community. God thinks you're worth it, too. So, let's not settle! Let's invite God into our journey, let's add value, let's not wish away our circumstances, let's run our race, let's put our heart out there, let's build, and then we will indeed move past the wishing.

You took a few minutes to dream about the answers to some questions earlier as you read, go back to those thoughts:

What do you envision for your life?
What type of person do you want to be?
What do you want your relationships (friends, family, marriage) to look like?

Now it is time to make some well laid-out plans.

Set some goals for upping your game in the study of the Word and in prayer. What, specially, are you going to do to set yourself up to be faithful in these spiritual disciplines?

The dreams that you gave words to in answer to the above questions are not just going to happen. Hard work will be involved! What are the first steps in each of these building projects?

Walk with the dreamers, the believers, the
courageous, the cheerful, the planners, the doers,
the successful people with their heads in the clouds
and their feet on the ground. Let their spirit
light a fire within you to leave this world
better than when you found it.

—*Wilfred Peters*

Conclusion

Dear Friends,

As you have read through these pages, it is my hope you have been inspired to move past the wishing. I want to encourage you to not let go of the idea of forming a Team Brave until it has been established and is being implemented in your life. This idea is a God-inspired concept that I know was placed in our hands to be shared with others. Brave, intentional living is best fostered in a group of like-hearted friends.

It is my prayer that you would have a Team Brave the rest of your life. The people you form your circle with will change, and that is okay. There will be seasons for different groups, with different goals. Don't be afraid to open your circle to add people. Encourage others to begin their own groups. My personal journey with my Team Brave has been life-changing, encouraging, and has brought joy to my friendships and a new dimension to my walk with Christ.

May you walk boldly in this one, amazing life you have been given. Remember, you are deeply loved, for all of time, no matter what by our Savior, Jesus Christ. He is with you on this journey. He will never leave you, nor forsake you. He has given you everything you need for the life you have.

Take courage, as you move past the wishing.

All my love…

Jen

Acknowledgements

This project is the sum of the efforts of many people and my heart is full of gratitude for each person who helped make this book possible.

I am so grateful for Team Brave and the beautiful journey we have been on this last year. I am so proud of each of you and the strides you have made. Thank you for teaching me so many beautiful life lessons as we have ventured to move past the wishing together.

Thank you to Elisabeth Willard and Lisa Seaton for your continuous encouragement from the moment this idea was formed. There were many times your life-giving words gave me just the push I needed to keep moving forward and believing this was possible.

Thank you to Erin Campbell for coming alongside and helping me form my words and thoughts when I needed to put more of me on the pages of this work. I'm grateful to have had your amazing insight and encouragement.

Thank you to Stacey Welch for lifting my arms and helping care for the treasures I hold dearest to my heart, my children. You made it possible for me to tuck away and pen this piece. I am truly grateful.

Thank you to my family for making me who I am today. Your support and encouragement makes my heart swell. My journey is beautiful because of the family I get to live it with.

To my boys, Caden, Connor, and Paxton—thank you for being patient with me while I took time to write. Caden and Connor, thank you for asking me about the book and being excited for it. You are the loves of my life and I can't believe I get to be your mom! You are my glorious adventure!

To my amazing husband, Jer—there are no words to describe my deep appreciation for you. You believed in me when I didn't believe in myself. You have always pushed me, knowing that God had a great purpose for me that I needed to discover. Thank you for helping me see and believe that purpose. You are my greatest inspiration. I love you beyond measure.

And finally, thank You to my Heavenly Father and Savior, Jesus Christ. Thank You doesn't sum up what all is in my heart. Words fall short, so simply put, I love You and I am deeply grateful for all You have given me. Life, and life to the fullest indeed.

Endnotes

Chapter One, Two, Four & Nine

Title: The Strongest Strong's Exhaustive Concordance of the Bible
Author: James Strong, John R. Kohlenberger III & James A. Swanson
Publisher: Zondervan; Revised edition (September 4, 2011)
http://www.zondervan.com/reference/concordances-dictionaries-language-re-
sources/the-strongest-strong-s-exhaustive-concordance-of-the-bible-larger-
print-edition

Chapter Four

"steward." *Dictionary.com* Unabridged. Random House, Inc. 20 Mar. 2015.
<Dictionary.com http://dictionary.reference.com/browse/steward>.